THE DIPLOMATIC KIDNAPPINGS

THE DIPLOMATIC KIDNAPPINGS
A REVOLUTIONARY TACTIC OF URBAN TERRORISM

by

CAROL EDLER BAUMANN

MARTINUS NIJHOFF/THE HAGUE/1973

PRINTED IN BELGIUM

TABLE OF CONTENTS

INTRODUCTION

The recent series of diplomatic kidnappings has produced some serious thinking not only in Washington but in most of the foreign offices and embassies throughout the diplomatic world. The kidnappings—and how to deal with them—have been the subject of Congressional committee hearings, State Department deliberations, and international debate and action by the Organization of American States. It is the purpose of this study to analyze them within the context of urban guerilla terrorism, international legal norms, and world diplomatic practice.

Selected examples of diplomatic kidnappings, particularly those in Latin America and Canada, strikingly illustrate the new revolutionary strategy of utilizing terrorism as a political tactic to achieve long-range political goals. As with its kindred phenomenon—the airplane hijackings—the kidnappings of foreign diplomats seize upon and exploit innocent victims as hostage pawns; a bargaining situation is thus created in which the revolutionary minority can achieve a diplomatic leverage which is far greater than in proportion to its numbers, military strength, or popular appeal. Through terrorism the urban guerillas hope to achieve tactical advances within the general strategy of political revolution; even temporary governmental repression if it occurs in reprisal becomes part of that strategy. Chapter I in particular and the entire manuscript in general examine the kidnappings within the parameters of revolutionary terrorism.

The kidnappings have also had serious legal and political ramifications in the realm of world diplomacy. In addition to their obvious infringements upon traditional diplomatic privileges and immunities, the kidnappings and assassinations of foreign emissaries have raised complex legal questions regarding state responsibility for the protection of aliens. In practical terms they have also created serious—and as yet unsolved—

security problems both for the sending and for the receiving states. Moreover, in attempting to secure "trades" of kidnapped diplomats for political prisoners and to obtain refuge for them in foreign states or embassies, the kidnappers have sparked both speculation and concern over the entire matter of diplomatic asylum and extradition—their rights and their limitations. Finally, as an effective technique of terrorism, the "diplonappings" have mobilized the diplomatic community in an effort to outlaw them as international crimes against humanity.

Any academic analysis of a hybrid legal/political problem of such immediate relevance to the practical conduct of international diplomacy requires a parallel examination of international law, international organizations, and international politics. It also requires some attention to the ways in which each of these aspects of diplomacy relates to the others and to the diplomatic kidnappings themselves. For example, just as international legal principles may be manipulated to support and justify national policies based upon political expediency, so the policy alternatives available to any state may also be limited and shaped by the legal rules and customs within which they are formulated. It is therefore essential to search for and to explore these interrelationships and to apply them to the specific cases of "diplonappings" which have recently taken place. This has been the purpose of Chapters II through VII.

When such an academic analysis presumes to venture beyond the exposition of the problem itself, however, and attempts to wrestle with actual policy alternatives, it becomes "policy-oriented" and subject to all the pitfalls of the real world of *Realpolitik*. In full recognition of the dangers those pitfalls can create, this study has been designed to combine the neutral objectivity of a scholarly analysis of the relevant rules of international law and diplomacy with the somewhat more involved and perhaps subjective judgments and policy recommendations necessitated by policy-oriented research. In Chapter VIII, therefore, it examines various policy alternatives which have been suggested as methods to control, if not totally prevent, the "diplonapping" spree. It suffers, as all topical research, from the lack of adequate official documentation and from the consequent need to rely heavily upon newspaper and other periodical accounts. Where this has appeared inadequate, additional information has been sought from the organizations, governments, and individuals concerned.

In conclusion, I wish to acknowledge the several contributions of those friends, colleagues, and students who assisted me along the path of publication.

My decision to develop what began as an article into a full book-length study was encouraged by Dr. Ralph K. Huitt, Director, National Association of State Universities and Land Grant Colleges. The book underwent its second metamorphosis from a quasi-legal orientation into a political/policy analysis with an emphasis upon the strategy of urban terrorism as a result of several discussions with Mr. Marian A. Czarnecki, Staff Consultant of the House Foreign Affairs Committee. I also want to thank my friends and colleagues, Professor Donald R. Shea and Professor David Fellman, both of whom not only read portions of the manuscript but offered many valuable comments on it. My indebtedness extends to many people, but intellectually to no one more than to Professor Llewellyn Pfankuchen who opened to me the many vistas of the world beyond Wisconsin.

For assistance in preparing the manuscript for publication, my thanks go to Helen C. Wenberg, Program Specialist at the Institute of World Affairs, and to Barbara Kuster, my secretary; thanks are also due to Nikola Kostich for his research help and to Chris Deily, Mike Callahan, and Tim Steinhoff, my student assistants.

Finally, I want to express my gratitude to my family—Richard, Dawn, and Wendy—who always knew I could do what I set out to do and encouraged me to believe so too.

The book is dedicated to the professional diplomatic corps throughout the world.

Carol Edler Baumann — 1972

Director, Institute of World Affairs
Professor, Department of Political Science
The University of Wisconsin-Milwaukee

CHAPTER I

URBAN TERRORISM IN REVOLUTIONARY STRATEGY

The diplomatic kidnappings, a relatively new phenomenon in world politics, have dramatized the growing prevalence of violence and terrorism as tactics of urban revolutionary strategy. The urban guerilla has emerged not only in Latin America, but in North America, Europe, and parts of North Africa and the Middle East as well, as the heir apparent to the peasant revolutionary of Mao, Castro, and Ché.[1] Yet urban and rural guerillas alike have shared a common heritage of 20th Century revolutionary theory which encompasses within it the role of guerilla warfare and the uses of terrorism. Tomes have been written and published on revolution itself, revolutionary theories, and revolutionaries; there is also a sizable collection of works on guerilla warfare *per se*. It is not the purpose of this chapter, therefore, even to attempt to summarize that body of literature, but rather to extract from it the relevant theories which have formed the literary matrix, so to speak, of the urban terrorist. It is particularly pertinent to seek out and examine those writings which have become the virtual guidelines to action for the modern revolutionary.

More than those of Marx and Engels, the works of Mao Tse-tung have had a wide appeal as strategic guidelines to guerilla warfare. Mao himself did not consider guerilla warfare to be the sole determining factor in achieving political control of a state, but he did regard it as a necessary component of an agrarian-based revolution.[2] Like others, Mao saw such a revolution as developing through various stages during which "direct action" becomes increasingly important. In the "second"

---

[1] Mao Tse-tung, Fidel Castro, and Ernesto Ché Guevara; theorists and practitioners of revolutionary guerilla warfare with an emphasis on peasant operations in the countryside.

[2] Griffith, Samuel B., *Mao Tse-tung: On Guerrilla Warfare*, p. 20. Frederick A. Praeger, New York, 1961.

phase of his strategy "acts of sabotage and terrorism multiply" and in order to "protect the revolution" the kidnapping of uncooperative landlords is suggested.[3] It should be noted that Mao also placed emphasis upon building up "mass" support for the movement in these early stages whereas the urban terrorists of today are somewhat divided on when and if such support should be sought.

Although early Communist revolutionary activities in China, patterned on the Soviet model, were concentrated in the cities, Mao did not personally favor this strategy and, when he attained a position of influence, he promoted revolution in the countryside with the peasants as his weapon and his target. It has been argued that Mao preferred the peasantry both because he himself came from peasant origins and therefore understood and trusted the peasant mentality which had been "uncorrupted" by foreign influences, and because he also understood the difficulties of promoting and achieving urban revolution in a predominantly rural China.[4] When urban insurrections failed in Shanghai and Canton in 1925-1927 and again in Changsa in 1930, Mao parted from those who had advocated them and developed his own concept of the peasant army and rural revolution. The Maoist strategy of guerilla warfare in the countryside has provided the classic model for most of the Asian revolutionary movements since 1945 and for many of the early Latin American revolutionaries prior to the appearance of the urban guerillas.

Less well-known internationally, but influential in Europe and North Africa in terms of his theory of anti-colonial revolutionary warfare involving the peasantry, is Frantz Fanon, theoretician and propagandist for the Algerian liberation movement. Fanon particularly emphasized the use of force and violence—both to overthrow colonial oppressors and to unify the rebel forces. Thus, he states: "...violence binds them together as a whole, since each individual forms a violent link in the great chain, a part of the great organism of violence which has surged upwards in reaction to the settler's violence in the beginning." [5] Like Mao, however, Fanon maintains that it is not the proletariat nor the urban middle class which will lead this violent revolution, but the

---

[3] *Ibid.*, p. 21.

[4] Said, Abdul A., and Collier, Daniel M., *Revolutionism*, pp. 16-17. Allyn and Bacon, Inc., Boston, 1971.

[5] Quoted in Wolf, Eric R., *Peasant Wars of the Twentieth Centry*, p. 244. Harper and Row, New York, 1969.

peasantry; even in the towns any support which might be mustered would also come primarily from the peasantry—from the landless peasants who had entered the cities in search of labor.[6]

A leading African theorist of revolutionary warfare is Kwame Nkrumah who in actively leading the anti-colonial struggle in Ghana developed his own approach to guerilla warfare in Africa. In his *Handbook of Revolutionary Warfare,* he set forth that approach in detail. Less concerned with the urban-rural dichotomy, Nkrumah bases the revolutionary struggle in Africa on both the workers and the peasants. He echoes Fanon's emphasis upon the need for violence to counteract the uses of violence by the imperialists to maintain their own control. Arguing that peaceful political action to achieve liberation has been proved ineffective, Nkrumah maintains that the people's armed struggle as "the highest form" of political action is a revolutionary catalyst in a neo-colonialist situation.[7] He distinguishes between zones under enemy control, contested zones, and liberated zones and states that the only missing link between the first two is "a handful of genuine revolutionaries prepared to organise and act." [8]

In his chapter dealing with the principles and techniques of guerilla warfare, Nkrumah outlines in great detail the concrete methods of guerilla organization, strategy and tactics in a manner strikingly similar to that of Carlos Marighella in his "Minimanual" for the urban guerilla. Thus, he proposes the establishment of centralized sections for recruitment, information, operations, sabotage, instruction, armament, provisions, health, propaganda, volunteers, and communications. As with Mao in rural China and Ché and Castro in Latin America, Nkrumah stresses both mobility and the ability to concentrate and disperse their forces as essential tactics of guerilla warfare. Devoting an entire section to propaganda as particularly important, he also stresses sabotage of the enemy's weak points and destruction of his "economic lifelines." In this, Nkrumah's instructions again parallel the tactics of the urban terrorists.

Of particular interest for the study of diplomatic kidnappings as a technique of terrorism are Nkrumah's rather astute observations regarding "imperialist" propaganda against revolutionary war in Africa as both

---

[6] *Ibid.,* p. 245.

[7] Nkrumah, Kwame, *Handbook of Revolutionary Warfare,* p. 52. International Publishers, New York, 1969.

[8] *Ibid.,* p. 49.

immoral and economically wasteful. Nkrumah counters that the African "armed struggle for freedom is neither moral nor immoral, it is a scientific historically-determined necessity." [9] Arguing that the colonialists and neo-colonialists have condemned *a priori* all African revolutionary activities to failure, he points out that in both press and radio accounts of African guerilla warfare the guerillas are always depicted as "terrorists" who are "poorly-trained, ill-equiped, demoralised and uncertain of the cause for which they are fighting."[10] Moreover, when such guerillas are captured, they are tried and treated as criminals and not as prisoners of war. So also, as will be seen, the Latin American terrorists have been regarded not as "political" prisoners, or "prisoners of war," but as common criminals.

In Latin America the revolutionary strategy of guerilla warfare as developed in theory and promulgated in practice by Fidel Castro and Ché Guevara and as publicized by Regis Debray has perhaps been the most influential of contemporary revolutionary models, at least prior to the emergence of its urban guerilla counterpart. Whether or not the Cuban revolution itself can be exported to other Latin American countries is less pertinent to this study than the fact that its strategy of guerilla warfare has been exported and has greatly influenced the thinking of Latin American revolutionaries. Although the political kidnappings have been utilized as a tactic of urban terrorism, terrorism as such has had its place in the strategy of both urban and rural guerillas. Because of this, it is appropriate to devote a few pages to the Castro model of guerilla warfare in rural zones and the creation of a mobile strategic force as the nucleus of a people's army and future socialist state.[11]

Regis Debray, through his book on *Revolution in the Revolution?* and other writings, has been widely recognized as a major publicist on the Cuban revolution and an unofficial spokesman for Castro's own thinking.[12] In *Revolution in the Revolution?* Debray particularly stresses: 1) the guerilla as central to the revolution, 2) the need to subordinate the cities to the countryside, and 3) the role of violence in revolutionary activ-

[9] *Ibid.*, p. 19.

[10] *Ibid.*, pp. 19-20.

[11] Debray, Regis, *Revolution in the Revolution?*, p. 24. Grove Press, Inc., New York, 1967.

[12] See Said and Collier, *op. cit.*, pp. 107-114, and Huberman, Leo, and Sweezy, Paul M. (Eds.), *Regis Debray and the Latin American Revolution.* Monthly Review Press, New York and London, 1968.

ities. Arguing that in the past Communist party subordination of guerilla groups to the party which itself had not changed its normal peacetime organization had produced a series of fatal military errors, Debray maintains that: "No political front which is basically a deliberative body can assume leadership of a people's war; only a technically capable executive group, centralized and united on the basis of identical class interests, can do so; in brief, only a revolutionary general staff." [13] Debray argues that since guerilla warfare is essentially political, political leadership should not and cannot be counterposed to military leadership. Rather, "...one cannot see how a political leadership, in the Latin America of today, can remain aloof from technical problems of war; it is equally inconceivable that there can be political cadres who are not simultaneously military cadres." [14] Thus, he concludes that although pure "politicians" who want to remain "pure" cannot lead the revolution, pure "military men" can do so, and by their experience in leading a guerilla group they become politicians as well.

Drawing largely upon the experiences of the Cuban revolution, Regis Debray thus theorizes that the guerilla movement itself first creates unity within its own ranks and then as it grows it creates rank-and-file unity among all parties and non-party elements and, "Eventually, the future People's Army will beget the party of which it is to be, theoretically, the instrument: essentially the party is the army." [15] He concludes in his chapter on "Principal Lesson for the Present" that the Cuban revolution has in fact made "a decisive contribution" to international revolutionary experience and to Marxism-Leninism: "Under certain conditions, the political and the military are not separate, but form one organic whole, consisting of the people's army, whose nucleus is the guerrilla army. The vanguard party can exist in the form of the guerrilla *foco* itself. The guerrilla force is the party in embryo." [16] This conclusion, he argues, has ended several decades' "divorce" between Marxist theory and revolutionary practice. After stating repeatedly that "The people's army will be the nucleus of the party, not vice versa," Debray stresses once again that "...insurrectional activity is today the number one political activity." [17]

---

[13] Debray, *op. cit.,* p. 86.
[14] *Ibid.,* p. 88.
[15] *Ibid.,* p. 105.
[16] *Ibid.,* p. 106.
[17] *Ibid.,* p. 116.

Debray's thesis has been widely criticized not so much because of its emphasis upon the importance of guerilla warfare, but because of its lack of an overall political framework or clear statement of policy goals: "Since a political framework is lacking and political philosophy is placed in a subordinate position, the goal will never be reached because it can never be recognized. The multiplication of the guerilla groups is a goal in itself in Debray's thought. Revolution is a tautology which exists for no other purpose, and Debray reflects the frustration inherent in this theory." [18] Moreover, although it may be quite true that political cadres must simultaneously be military cadres, it does not follow that a guerilla force automatically becomes "political" purely because it is military.[19] Though Debray stresses revolutionary guerilla warfare, he is notably silent on the purposes of that warfare and the political programs of the party which will arise out of the armed vanguard of revolutionaries. This stands in stark contrast not only to Mao who realized that political goals must determine the strategy of revolution, but also to Ché Guevara who emphasized that : "Above all it must be made clear that this type of struggle is a method: a method for achieving a purpose. That purpose, indispensable and unavoidable for every revolutionary, is the conquest of political power. Therefore, in analyses of specific situations in the different Latin America (sic) countries the concept of the guerrilla force must be applied within the simplest terms of the struggle to achieve that purpose." [20]

Debray also differed from both Mao and Ché in his lack of concern for mobilizing the power of the peasantry behind these revolutionary activities. As will be seen, he stressed the countryside over the city as the locus of his guerilla cadres, but failed to provide any program for organizing the populace of the countryside behind the guerilla bands. In the initial phase of the revolution, in fact, Debray actually argued against any close association with the peasantry—"the guerrilla force is *independent* of the civilian population." [21] Even recognizing that

[18] Said and Collier, *op. cit.,* p. 108.

[19] See Silva, Clea, "The Errors of the Foco Theory" in Huberman, Leo, and Sweezy, Paul M. (Eds.), *Regis Debray and the Latin American Revolution,* p. 26. Monthly Review Press, New York and London, 1968.

[20] Ché Guevara, "Guerrilla Warfare: A Method" in Gerassi, John (Ed.), *Venceremos!,* p. 266. Simon and Schuster, New York, 1968.

[21] See reference to this point in Worsley, Peter, "Guevara and Debray" in Huberman and Sweezy, *op. cit.,* pp. 132-4.

Debray did envision the ultimate association of the guerillas with the peasants living in guerilla-controlled areas, his general lack of attention to guerilla/peasant relationships contrasts both with Mao ("We must go to the masses; arouse them to activity; concern ourselves with their weal and woe;" and "We should make the broad masses realize that we represent their interests, that our life and theirs are intimately interwoven.") [22] and with Ché ("A guerrilla war is a people's war, and it *is* a mass struggle. To attempt to conduct this type of war without the support of the populace is a prelude to inevitable disaster. The guerrilla force is the people's fighting vanguard, located in a specific part of a given territory ... It is supported by the masses of peasants and workers of the region and the entire territory in question. Except on this basis, guerilla warfare is unacceptable.") [23]

Despite these differences, however, Debray's emphasis upon guerilla warfare itself as the vehicle for achieving revolutionary change is equally central to the theories of Ché. Thus, in his article on "Guerrilla Warfare: A Method," Ché argues that both the "objective conditions" in Latin America—the conditions of exploitation, awareness among the masses, the world crisis of imperialism, and a worldwide revolutionary movement—and the "subjective conditions"—an awareness of the need for change and the certainty of the possibility of change—are ripe for armed struggle. Basing his analysis of guerilla warfare on these premises, Ché maintains "the necessity of guerrilla action in Latin America as the central axis of the struggle." [24] The arguments which determine that necessity, Ché continues, are the need to destroy "the oppressor's army" through the opposition of a people's army, the general situation of the Latin American peasants, and, finally, the hemisphere-wide character of the struggle in which the Andes are to become in Castro's phrase "the Sierra Maestra" of South America.

The second major element of Debray's theory of revolution in Latin America—the need to subordinate the cities to the countryside—is shared both by Ché and by Castro. Pointing to the contributions of the Cuban revolution to the revolutionary movements of Latin America, Ché writes that in underdeveloped Latin American states, the arena of the armed struggle should be fundamentally in the country.[25] Admitting

---

[22] Quoted in *ibid.*, pp. 132-3.
[23] Ché Guevara, "Guerrilla Warfare: A Method" in Gerassi, *op. cit.*, p. 267.
[24] *Ibid.*, p. 273.
[25] *Ibid.*, p. 267.

that urban forces can perform actions of incalculable importance, Ché nonetheless maintains that the destruction of such forces would not mean the end of the "heart" of the revolution, the leadership. Rather, "From its rural fortress, the latter would continue to act as a catalyst of the revolutionary spirit of the masses and organize new forces for other battles." [26] Fidel Castro put it even more bluntly when he said, "The city is a cemetery of revolutionaries and resources." [27] Or, again, "The most fitting slogan of the day ought to be, *All guns, all bullets, and all resources to the Sierra.*" [28]

Debray bases his own theoretical subordination of the city to the countryside almost completely on the experiences of the Cuban revolution and the *dicta* of Fidel. Moreover, it flows logically from his major emphasis upon the guerilla *foco* themselves as the vanguard of the revolution and embryo of a future party. Writing of Castro's strategy in Cuba,[29] Debray states that Fidel placed his main emphasis upon the consolidation of the rural guerillas on whom the leadership of the national movement devolved. The movement in Havana was to be placed under the leadership of a rural force which in January, 1957, consisted of only twenty men. All available arms were to be sent to the Sierra Maestra and not a single one to be diverted to urban resistance. Although this strategy led to conflict with the urban wing of the movement, Debray maintains that it permitted the creation of the mobile strategic force, the Rebel Army, in the shortest time possible. In contrast, he argues, if political leadership remains in the city it will be debilitated, destroyed, or dismantled. His theme strikes again and again at the rigidity of the Communist party urban-based organizations in Latin America and their inability to assume an active lead of the revolutionary movement.

Debray maintains that the "descent into the city," as he calls it, is fraught with several dangers for the guerillas who face there "... a deadly risk. Sooner or later the guerrilla leader will fall." [30] As has been aptly pointed out,[31] such a view overlooks the fact that risks exist both in urban and rural guerilla operations; moreover, the "betrayal"

[26] *Ibid., p. 274.*
[27] Quoted in Debray, *op. cit.,* p. 69.
[28] *Ibid.,* p. 76.
[29] *Ibid.,* p. 76.
[30] *Ibid.,* p. 68.
[31] See both Silva, "The Errors of the Foco Theory" and Petras, James, "Debray: Revolutionary or Elitist?" in Huberman and Sweezy, *op. cit.,* pp. 27-29 and 112-113.

of guerillas in the cities to which Debray refers was due less to the urban locale of the political leadership than to its policies which either failed to provide adequate protection for them or lacked the underground organization to do so. In his implication that the urban "politicos," immersed in the political life of "good times," know nothing of the war and its problems, Debray has been strongly attacked by the counterargument that an urban underground existence is itself hardly a *dolce vita.* Although one of his critics agrees with Debray as to the existential problems of isolation, fear and neurosis, and loss of identity which impinge upon the urban underground activist, he points out that rural guerillas face similar neuroses in their separation from family, insecurity of constant mobility, and pressures of war and military discipline. He concludes that: "...one form is no more or less formative or deformative than another; that the task of being a revolutionary in the country or in the city does violence to the individual; and that a revolutionary can transcend this threat of self-violence only if he possesses a clear idea of why he does violence to himself, what he is giving his life to—in sum, when he perceives the full grandeur of the cause." [32]

Ché Guevara, as Castro and Debray, regarded guerilla warfare in the countryside as the primary method of revolution in Latin America, but he did deal briefly with urban or " suburban warfare" in his book on *Guerrilla Warfare.* Stating that suburban guerilla bands can never spring up of their own accord but will be born only after certain conditions necessary for their survival have been created, Ché maintained that the suburban guerillas should always be under the direct orders of chiefs located in another zone. Moreover, the function of urban guerilla bands would not be to carry out independent actions but to coordinate their activities with overall strategic plans so as to support the action of larger groups in other areas. The suburban groups should be small—four to five men—"...because the suburban guerrilla must be considered as situated in exceptionally unfavorable ground, where the vigilance of the enemy will be much greater and the possibilities of reprisals as well as of betrayal are increased enormously."[33] Emphasizing the importance of discipline and discretion in such a situation, Ché nonetheless concluded that the importance of suburban struggle has usually been underestimated and is really very great: "A good operation

---

[32] Silva, *ibid.,* p. 29.

[33] Ché Guevara, Ernesto, *Guerrilla Warfare,* p. 37. Monthly Review Press, New York and London, 1961.

of this type extended over a wide area paralyzes almost completely the commercial and industrial life of the sector and places the entire population in a situation of unrest, of anguish, almost of impatience for the development of violent events that will relieve the period of suspense." [34]

The third theme of Regis Debray deals with the role of violence in any revolution. As with his rural bias, Debray's preoccupation with violence flows from his basic emphasis upon guerilla warfare as central to the revolution itself. Regarding guerilla warfare as the only way to achieve change in Latin America, Debray propounds a strategy of violence divorced from any political framework or theory. Political activity and the political process are ignored at best and scorned as productive of little or nothing. Debray's answer to the social and economic injustices of Latin America is not the ballot box but the bullet: "A successful ambush, a torturer cut down, a consignment of arms captured—they are the best answers to any reformist faint-heartedness which may arise in one or another American country." [35] Normal political activity, in fact, is regarded as a hindrance to the extreme militant revolutionary who must act and not talk.

Without the framework of a comprehensive theory as to the purposes or goals of the revolution, however, Debray's strategy of violence exists in a sort of political void or vacuum. Thus, although it can be maintained that "Violence may be used extensively in order to achieve its political goals; yet, when used without political structure, violence becomes an end in itself." [36] Debray, it has been argued, fails as a revolutionist theoretician for precisely the reason that he does not provide this political structure for the violence which he advocates. Rather, he emphasizes "violence *qua* violence as means, values, and goals." [37] Unlike Mao and Ché who stressed guerilla warfare as the military means to achieve political power, Debray appears to regard armed struggle as a goal and value in itself. Moreover, as Fanon, Debray tends to perceive of violence as a necessary catalyst not only for the revolution itself but for the creation of the revolutionary guerilla—a catalyst which binds him to his guerilla comrades and in a sense embues itself with an almost moral aura.

[34] *Ibid.,* p. 38.
[35] Debray, *op. cit.,* p. 126.
[36] Said and Collier, *op. cit.,* p. 109.
[37] *Ibid.,* p. 112.

In his writings on violence, however, Debray does deal with terrorism in the cities. Again concerned with subordination of the cities to the countryside, Debray argues that if the guerilla force is not recognized as the directive force of the revolutionary movement, the results are "independent and anarchic" actions in the cities which can jeopardize not only the guerillas' plans but also the significance of the battle itself. If, on the other hand, city terrorism is subordinate to the "fundamental struggle" in the countryside, it does have a strategic value from a military point of view: "...it immobilizes thousands of enemy soldiers, it ties up most of the repressive mechanism in unrewarding tasks of protection: factories, bridges, electric generators, public buildings, highways, oil pipe-lines—these can keep busy as much as three quarters of the army. The government must, since it is the government, protect everywhere the interests of property owners; the *guerrilleros* don't have to protect anything anywhere." [38] Therefore, the relationship of guerilla forces to government forces is not a purely arithmetical one. But despite its strategic value, Debray says, city terrorism cannot assume any "decisive" role and does entail certain political dangers.

At this point, it is necessary to turn from the specific writings of Regis Debray and to examine some of the more developed theories of violence in general and terrorism in particular. Despite the existence of some nonviolent revolutionary activities, most contemporary revolutionary theories and experiences tend to stress the uses of violence in order to achieve political power.[39] In Latin America, the prevalence of revolutionary violence has been related to what has been termed the "political culture" of violence in many Latin American political systems. Contrasting them to relatively nonviolent political systems in the United States and Britain, "...many Latin American political systems are characterized by manifestly violent political behavior and acceptance of violence as a 'legitimate' means for the pursuit of power." [40] In his article on "Violence and Politics in Latin America," Merle Kling refers not only to the frequency of revolution (at least forty successful revolutions

---

[38] Debray, *op. cit.,* p. 75.

[39] Said and Collier, *op. cit.,* p. 63. See also Needler, Martin C., *Political Development in Latin America: Instability, Violence, and Evolutionary Change,* Chapter III: The Purposes of Violence. Random House, New York, 1968.

[40] Kling, Merle, "Violence and Politics in Latin America" in Horowitz, de Castro, Gerassi (Eds.), *Latin American Radicalism,* p. 193. Random House, Inc., New York, 1969.

between 1950 and 1965), but to the pervasiveness of political violence (including warfare, turmoil, rioting, terrorism, mutiny and coups) which does not culminate in revolution; he concludes that, "In the light of the evidence, political violence cannot be regarded as aberrant behavior in Latin America. It is recurring, chronic, and rule-conforming..." [41]

Kling enumerates the legal concomitants of Latin American patterns of violence as: "(1) frequent replacement and revision of written constitutional documents; (2) conspicuous departures from prescribed constitutional norms in political behavior; (3) recurrent suspensions of constitutional guarantees, declarations of states of siege, and the conduct of government by decree; and (4) the institutionalization of procedures for exile, including the right of asylum." [42] Moreover, he points to such nonpolitical and cultural socialization influences (such as the cult of *machismo* and acceptance of death) as sources contributing to behavior patterns of political violence. Finally, Kling maintains that the roles and backgrounds of Latin American "experts in violence" are extremely diffuse and that the goals which they seek are equally diverse; thus, both the range of their policy interests and the range of possible revolutionary outcomes are exceedingly broad. Within this sort of matrix of political violence the role of terrorism in Latin America, at least, assumes its proper proportions.

In practice, violent revolutionaries seek changes which they believe are impossible to achieve without control of government. Moreover, they believe that they cannot gain that control by peaceful means; hence, there is no alternative to violence. Many Latin American one-time reformers have reached the conclusion that the only way to break the structure of government—or the system—is by violent revolution. For example, Fabricio Ojeda, once a student reformer who sought change in Venezuela through the electoral process and who then became a revolutionary guerilla and was killed in jail in 1966, wrote in "Toward Revolutionary Power": "Nonrevolutionary politicians think that everything stems from the majority vote needed to win the government. They think that if a democratic representative government is formed, and if it aims at the total enforcement of the law, no one would dare challenge the law. They have not yet understood—and this comes out in all their statements—that in order to exercise real power, force is required; force

---

[41] *Ibid.*, p. 196.
[42] *Ibid.*, p. 200.

that is able to confront and successfully defeat the reactionary classes affected by constitutional change." [43]

Castro himself has propounded the theme of violence on several occasions. Stating that the ruling classes in Latin America have actually organized the state so as to maintain themselves in power by all possible means, Castro argued that those who believe a take-over through elections is possible are simply "supernaive"; or again, that "those who assert anywhere in Latin America that they will take over power peacefully will be deceiving the masses." [44] Ernesto Ché Guevara has echoed Castro's thoughts even more graphically: "...the present moment may or may not be the proper one for starting the struggle, but we cannot harbor any illusions, and we have no right to do so, that freedom can be obtained without fighting. And the battles will not be mere street fights with stones against tear-gas bombs, nor pacific general strikes; neither will they be those of a furious people destroying in two or three days the repressive superstructure of the ruling oligarchies. The struggle will be long, harsh, ..." [45] In addition, Ché emphasized the emotional significance of hatred as a necessary element of the struggle—"relentless hatred of the enemy that impels us over and beyond the natural limitations of man and transforms us into effective, violent, selective, and cold killing machines. Our soldiers must be thus; a people without hatred cannot vanquish a brutal enemy. We must carry the war as far as the enemy carries it: to his home, to his centers of entertainment, in a total war." [46]

Ché also wrote about the role of terrorism in revolutionary warfare. After distinguishing between acts of sabotage as highly effective methods of warfare and acts of terrorism, Ché argued that the latter were generally ineffective and indiscriminate in their results, often making victims of innocent people. Terrorism could thus be considered a valuable tactic when used to murder some noted leader of "the oppressing forces," but not to kill persons "of small importance" since it often brings on retaliation by an increase of reprisals, including the deaths of the revolutionaries themselves. Moreover, by provoking police oppression, terrorist activities indirectly hinder contact between guerilla leaders and

[43] Ojeda, Fabricio, "Toward Revolutionary Power" in Horowitz, de Castro, and Gerassi (Eds.), *op cit.*, p. 645.

[44] Castro, Fidel, "Waves of the Future" in *ibid.*, p. 553.

[45] Ché Guevara, "Message to the Tricontinental" in *ibid.*, p. 617.

[46] *Ibid.*, p. 618.

the masses and thus make impossible the unification necessary for ultimate mass action. In general, Ché urged caution and circumspection in any uses of terrorism and its clear subordination to the political purposes of the revolution.[47]

Ché's distinction between the necessity for violence—fighting and hatred—in revolutionary warfare and his injunction against indiscriminate terrorism is, however, a fine one and not generally shared by other theorists of violence and terrorism. In fact, violence is an implicit or explicit aspect of the definition of terrorism, and terrorism a specific technique of revolutionary violence. Terror is thus used "to influence political behavior by extra-normal means" including the use or threat of violence; it is both the product of and contributing cause to "an atmosphere of fear and despair." [48] Just as there have been revolutions without violence, so there have also been revolutions without terror, yet terror and terrorist tactics have frequently been employed in revolutionary situations—both by desperate governments and by desperate insurgents. They are used as extranormal means of persuasion and coercion because: "There are things that cannot be accomplished *within the system by the rules of the system*; only by some extraordinary, extralegal, extra-normal process can they be effectuated. The creation of an atmosphere of despair breaks down the resistance of those who need to be persuaded; they are to be so shocked and numbed, so weakened and demoralized, and so pessimistic of hope that they become amenable to anything that promises release from tension. It is possible for agitators to produce such despair in the minds of the ruling elite or in those of the mass; it is also sometimes possible for a government to destroy an opposition by terror rather than to mollify it by more normal political methods." [49]

Although terrorism has not been the normal *modus operandi* of Latin American revolutionaries in the past, violence has been and, as has been suggested, terrorism is one type of violence and one technique of violent revolution. Nonetheless, it is clearly a supplementary technique and seldom a decisive one. Moreover, it is difficult to predict the results of the uses of terrorism which may be "a psychological weapon of unbelievable power," [50] but may also provoke harsh retaliation and

[47] Ché Guevara, *Guerrilla Warfare*, p. 26.

[48] Leiden, Carl, and Schmitt, Karl M. (Eds.), *The Politics of Violence*, p. 30. Prentice-Hall, Inc., Englewood Cliffs, N.J., 1968.

[49] *Ibid.*, pp. 31-32.

[50] Statement by Jacques Soustelle when Governor General of Algeria. Quoted in Crozier, Brian, *The Rebels*, p. 176. Beacon Press, Boston, 1960.

counter-terrorism in return. It has been argued that despite its obvious pitfalls terrorism has been increasingly resorted to by revolutionaries as "necessary" unless their cause quickly gains the open support of a majority of the population; in practice, it has therefore become a major strategy of revolutionary warfare.[51]

Terrorism is frequently employed when the terrain is not suitable and/or the political and military organization of an insurgent group is not developed sufficiently for total guerilla warfare;[52] or it is used as a supplement to that warfare. Thus, in towns and cities where "traditional" guerilla warfare is difficult, terrorism has erupted as the weapon of the urban guerilla. For the purposes of revolution, however, terrorism has generally been regarded as "a weapon of weakness" and in his study of counter-revolutionary war, John McCuen concludes that "...terrorism is not an efficient type of warfare. The revolutionaries cannot gain permanent support of a population by terror. Terror may ... drive people into support of the administration if the governing authorities can offer them security. The wise revolutionaries will dispense with terrorism as rapidly as possible to avoid this ultimately adverse reaction."[53] A similar conclusion was reached by Lewis Gann in his book, *Guerrillas in History*. Writing of the difficulties encountered by the urban guerilla, Gann concluded that terror has proved to be no substitute for victory: "Back-alley killings may depress morale and weaken the waverers for a time. But terror must be transmuted into political power. As long as the people remain convinced that the government will win in the end, violence of the ganster type is apt to yield diminishing returns."[54]

Despite these weaknesses of terror as a revolutionary weapon and the dangers inherent in guerilla warfare in the city, it has become increasingly evident that urban guerilla terrorism is definitely a current tactic, if not the long term norm, of revolutionary strategy, particularly in Latin America. Since the fall of Ché Guevara in the countryside of Bolivia, the *ciudad/sierra* or city/country juxtaposition of Regis Debray and his emphasis upon the latter have been more closely scrutinized and questioned and, if not repudiated, at least not followed in practice.

[51] McCuen, John J., *The Art of Counter-Revolutionary War*, p. 31. Stackpole Books, Harrisburg, Penn., 1966.

[52] *Ibid.*, p. 32.

[53] *Ibid.*, p. 33.

[54] Gann, Lewis H., *Guerrillas in History*, pp. 83-84. Hoover Institution Press, Stanford, California, 1971.

Thus, in 1968 it was the urban National Liberation Action band which mounted a campaign of "violence, radicalism, and terrorism" as an action-oriented revolutionary force in Brazil. Beginning with urban terrorism, the A.L.N. looked to rural guerilla warfare as the next stage of its revolutionary struggle. In the same year the Rebel Armed Forces began its spree of urban terrorism in Guatemala, and in Uruguay the highly organized Tupamaros moved from city bank robberies and thefts to bombings and kidnappings. Finally, in Canada and in Turkey it was not in the countryside or in the mountains that terrorism grew, but in the streets and alleys of Quebec and Ankara.

What are some of the reasons for this revolutionary movement to the cities? Recognizing the dangers of urban guerilla warfare such as the risks of exposure, relative concentration of government forces, and predominance of night-time operations, Gann has nonetheless also pointed to some developments which have somewhat facilitated the role of the urban terrorist.[55] The growth of an increasingly affluent working class and intelligentsia has permitted the purchase of cars, trucks, and communications equipment (radios, walkie-talkies, etc.) by terrorist groups. Cars have given the same mobility to the urban guerilla which has been the key to past success for his country cousin. Cities have the technicians and facilities available for producing and servicing the weapons and other equipment used by terrorist bands. They also have the mass media which can be manipulated both for propaganda purposes and for mobilization of crowds—and riots. The gangster/terrorist parallel is a surprisingly useful one for it calls to mind both the furtiveness and illegality of their mutual operations and the vastness and complexity of city life which provides the anonymity within which they can survive.

Another major factor contributing to the spread of urban terrorism is urbanization itself. Whereas the Mao-Castro emphasis upon the countryside as the focus for a rural revolution may well have suited the Chinese and Cuban situations, all Latin America is not China—nor is it Cuba. In Brazil alone there are five cities of over one million people each, two of them with more than five million each. According to Worsley,

...in Argentina, 70 percent of the population is urban; 600,000 people live in the *barriadas* around Lima, a city of one and a half million inhabitants; a so-called "primate city," like Guatemala City, embraces a fifth of the entire population of the country. Nor do these people necessarily have work.[56]

---

[55] *Ibid.*, p. 82.
[56] Worsley, "Guevara and Debray" in Huberman and Sweezy, *op. cit.*, p. 135.

He points out that this combination of high density population with severe unemployment is obviously politically volatile. It is hardly the middle class *status quo* supporters, but the landless peasantry and out of work laborers who are highly susceptible to revolutionary propaganda and to the call for urban action.

That call was iterated no more eloquently and movingly than by Carlos Marighella, the Brazilian urban terrorist who founded the National Liberation Action in 1968. Like Regis Debray, Marighella strongly criticized the established Communist organizations who continued to apply worn-out formulas and to argue that the "objective conditions" for revolution were not yet ripe. Also like Debray, Marighella based his strategy on the necessity for armed struggle under the leadership of a guerilla command. In his view, however, that struggle should be carried on by both rural and *urban* guerilla warfare. Recognizing the geographic and demographic factors peculiar to Brazil, he argued that the "guerrilla axes" of action should be based in the Guanabara-São Paulo-Belo Horizonte triangle—"the heart of Brazil."

Beginning with scattered bank robberies and isolated acts of sabotage, Marighella's guerilla band and others embarked upon their program of action projected in his own words: "Revolutionary groups can join together or act separately, with or without ties to each other. The important fact is action. That is what will awaken revolutionary energy among our people..." [57] His emphasis upon action was also epitomized in the name chosen for his revolutionary movement—the National Liberation Action. The A.L.N. was created as a result of the increasingly apparent need somehow to unify the disparate efforts of different groups in various parts of the country and consolidate them into one organization. As Marighella's activities spread, his early anonymity was lost and in November, 1968, the Guanabara police positively identified him as directing an assault on an armored bank car; Marighella was pronounced public enemy number one with a price placed on his head. A year later he was killed in a police ambush—in action.

It is apparent from his writings and a short biography of his life that Marighella's ultimate goal was the seizure of political power in Brazil by armed struggle. Although the actual policies to be pursued by a national liberation government were never specified in any great

---

[57] Quoted in Ferreira, J. Camara, *Carlos Marighella,* pp. 13-14. Tricontinental, Havana, Cuba, 1970.

detail,[58] it was nonetheless clear that economic reformation, social justice, and an end to "Yankee imperialism" were priority objectives. Like Ché and Castro, he regarded the struggle in Brazil as only part of a continental revolutionary movement: "There is no other way out for the Third World except the organization of a just and necessary war against imperialism." [59]

Although Marighella was a long-time member of the Brazilian Communist Party and became a member of the Executive Committee of the Central Committee of the Party in 1953, he became increasingly radicalized and committed to armed revolutionary struggle. Again reminiscent of Regis Debray, Marighella's criticisms of party inactivity and doctrinal sterility became more open and more frequent; at the end of 1966 he resigned from the Executive Committee to devote his entire time to revolutionary action. In his letter of resignation, Marighella voiced his criticisms stringently: "What makes the Executive Committee ineffectual is its lack of mobility" and absence of influence in basic industries and among the peasantry. "Executive work has been limited to holding meetings, writing up political notes, and preparing reports. Thus there is no planned action, no activity centered around the struggle." [60]

In addition, whereas the Party had come to believe in the possibility of a peaceful solution through the electoral process, Marighella argued that in Brazil the solution could only be armed struggle, the revolutionary road. Thus, he charged, "After so much rhetoric about how the violence of the ruling classes must be met with the violence of arms, nothing has been done to make words match deeds." [61] Echoing the cry of Castro in Cuba, Marighella stressed repeatedly his own conviction that the struggle for basic reform could not take place peacefully, but would occur only through the revolutionary seizure of power. In contrast to this approach and the development of a mass revolutionary movement, the Communist Party in Brazil had become a "peaceful party," suitable to electoral compromises and agreements. These were the Party "deformations" which Marighella opposed and which finally caused him to leave the Party.

---

[58] See "Perspectives for the Brazilian Revolution" in *ibid.*, pp. 96-97, for his proposed "Program for Unity."
[59] Quoted in "His Biography" in *ibid.*, p. 23.
[60] "Letter of Resignation" in *ibid.*, p. 34.
[61] *Ibid.*, p. 42.

Sparked by Marighella, revolutionary activities spread in the large cities of Brazil throughout 1968—in urban guerilla warfare and in psychological warfare which he regarded as the forerunners of rural guerilla warfare. As the guerilla forces themselves multiplied and political support for their diversified actions grew, they gradually unified and evolved into the National Liberation Action. In assessing the results of these first revolutionary actions, Marighella pointed to growth both in men and in firepower, to the creation of a national organization, and to the spread of the revolution by beginning with urban guerilla and psychological warfare instead of rural warfare. Working with the student movement which was engaged in street fighting at this time, the A.L.N. stimulated urban revolutionary actions throughout the country and, Marighella contended, provoked the enemy forces into fighting "a full-scale revolutionary war." [62] The government retaliated with Institutional Act No. 5 which, aimed against these revolutionary activities, defined them as including terrorism, attacks on banks and garrisons, and seizures of weapons and explosives. This, and other repressive measures, Marighella argued, simply fostered even greater popular discontent.

In addition to action, Marighella and the A.L.N. developed their own revolutionary strategy of guerilla warfare for Brazil—a three-phase strategy of planning and preparation, "unleashing," and, finally, shifting from guerilla to conventional warfare. The revolutionary struggle itself is fought by both urban and rural guerillas and by psychological warfare. Although Marighella maintained that their main effort was directed toward the rural guerilla and the development of a guerilla infrastructure wherever revolutionary organizations might appear, the A.L.N. had nonetheless begun with *urban* guerilla actions—attacking the interests of national and foreign capitalists, creating a climate of insecurity and uncertainty for the government, and demoralizing the military forces. However, Marighella viewed this urban beginning as leading to direct armed struggle against the large landowners by rural guerillas. Thus, an armed alliance of workers, peasants and students would spread the revolution through mobile guerilla forces throughout the country and project it to its final phase of conventional warfare, the conquest of power, and the establishment of a people's revolutionary government. [63] Marighella's detailed analysis of urban guerilla warfare and its strategy as set forth in his *Minimanual of the Urban Guerrilla* stands out as of

[62] Marighella, "Justification of a Thesis" in *ibid.*, p. 59.
[63] *Ibid.*, pp. 80-81.

particular interest for the purposes of this study. He defines the urban guerilla as a man who fights the military dictatorship "for his country's liberation" with arms and unconventional methods within the large Brazilian cities. Marighella distinguishes the urban guerilla from outlaws in that "The urban guerilla follows a political goal and only attacks the government, the big capitalists, and the foreign imperialists, particularly North Americans." [64] As an implacable enemy of the government, he systematically inflicts damage on the authorities and on those who dominate the country and exercise power. In Marighella's terms, the principal task of the urban guerilla is "to distract, to wear out, to demoralize" government forces and "to attack and destroy the wealth and property" of domestic and foreign capitalists. Finally, "The urban guerilla is not afraid of dismantling and destroying the present Brazilian economic, political, and social system, for his aim is to help the rural guerilla and to collaborate in the creation of a totally new and revolutionary social and political structure, with the armed people in power." [65]

Although several pages of the "Minimanual" are devoted to such matters as the personal qualities and life style of the urban guerrilla, as well as to such technical topics as preparation, firearms and firing groups, logistics and operations ("All You Wanted to Know About the Urban Guerilla" would be an apt subtitle), the objective and techniques of urban guerilla warfare are perhaps of most relevance here. Marighella points out that within the framework of the overall revolutionary struggle, two essential objectives for the urban guerilla are the physical liquidation of chiefs and assistants of the armed forces and police and the expropriation of government and capitalist resources.[66] The guerilla's continued existence itself is dependent upon both. In Brazil the number of such violent acts as political or military assassinations, fires and explosions, seizures of weapons and ammunition, assaults on banks and prisons, and the political kidnappings themselves have borne witness to the fact that Marighella's advice did not go unheeded.

The small four- to five-man "firing group" is another feature of the "Minimanual" which has had its apparent impact on the technique of diplonapping. Emphasizing flexibility, Marighella argues the right—in fact, the duty—of every firing group to exercise its own initiative: "...

---

[64] Marighella, Carlos, *Minimanual of the Urban Guerrilla,* p. 17. Tricontinental, Havana, Cuba, 1970.

[65] *Ibid.*

[66] *Ibid.,* p. 20.

except for the priority of objectives set by the strategic command, any firing group can decide to assault a bank, to kidnap or to execute an agent of the dictatorship, a figure identified with the reaction, or a North American spy, and can carry out any kind of propaganda or war of nerves against the enemy without the need to consult the general command." [67] This contrasts strikingly with Ché's injunction against independent actions by suburban guerilla bands. But for Marighella, "who is doing what" is less important than to increase the total volume of urban guerilla activities. This relative independence and multiplication of urban actions have been well exemplified in the activities of the highly organized Tupamaros in Uruguay, the F.A.R. (Rebel Armed Forces) in Guatemala, and the A.L.N. itself in Brazil. They were also a distinctive feature of the operations of the F.L.Q. (Le Front de Libération du Quebec) in the Canadian kidnappings of James Cross and Pierre Laporte.

Turning to the urban guerilla's techniques in general, Marighella emphasizes their aggressive and offensive nature, the elements of attack and retreat, and the function of demoralizing and distracting the enemy so as to permit "the emergence and survival of rural guerrilla warfare which is destined to play the decisive role in the revolutionary war." [68] Stressing the need for surprise, knowledge of the terrain, mobility and speed, information, and capacity for quick decisions, Marighella outlines the immediate objectives of urban guerilla action in Brazil, and then continues with a list "action models" of which approximately half will be examined briefly here: liberation of prisoners, executions, kidnappings, sabotage, terrorism, armed propaganda, and the "war of nerves."

"The liberation of prisoners is an armed operation designed to free the jailed urban guerrilla." [69] It is, of course, because of the difficulty of this task and the relative lack of success in accomplishing it by raids, assaults, and ambushes, that revolutionary bands have now turned to the technique of diplonapping as an alternative—using the kidnapped diplomat as a pawn to exchange for the release of jailed prisoners. This alternative, as will be demonstrated, has enjoyed almost instant success and only in a few cases up to the present time has it met with an adamant "no ransom" policy. "Execution" of spies, government or police agents, torturers and informers is also proposed by Marighella. It has been resorted to in practice in the cases of at least two kidnappings

[67] *Ibid.,* pp. 27-28.
[68] *Ibid.,* p. 30.
[69] *Ibid.,* p. 43.

—Ambassador von Spreti in Guatemala and Dan A. Mitrione in Uruguay —when ransom demands for the release of prisoners were outrightly rejected.

Sabotage, armed propaganda, and terrorism are all designed to create "the war of nerves" advocated by Marighella. In his "Minimanual," he not only spells out in detail how the urban guerilla can achieve the objective of sabotage in order to hurt, damage, make useless, or destroy vital enemy points, but he also identifies what those vital points are. Armed propaganda based on coordinated guerilla actions is aimed both at the government (demoralization) and at the populace (agitation and support). It has been consistently resorted to by the diplonappers and has, in fact, frequently figured as part of their ransom demands—publication of a manifesto, mass media attention to the kidnapping itself, etc. Terrorism, in turn, may encompass any of the above, as well as assaults, raids, ambushes, street riots, and seizures of weapons or ammunition. As Marighella states, "Terrorism is an arm the revolutionary can never relinquish." [70] All of these techniques together culminate in what Marighella terms "the war of nerves" or aggressive psychological warfare which uses the mass media to demoralize the government: "The object of the war of nerves is to misinform, spreading lies among the authorities, ...thus creating an air of nervousness, discredit, insecurity, uncertainty, and concern on the part of the government." [71]

In addition, Marighella specifically recommends kidnapping—capturing and holding in secret a police agent, North American spy, political personality, or notorious enemy of the revolutionary movement—as a technique used "to exchange or liberate imprisoned revolutionary comrades, or to force suspension of torture in the jail cells..." [72] Moreover, he maintains that the kidnapping of North American residents or visitors in Brazil affords a way to protest the penetration and domination of "United States imperialism" in Brazil. He obviously followed his own advice in the case of Ambassador C. Burke Elbrick, the United States Ambassador kidnapped by the A.L.N. in September, 1968. The details of the Elbrick case will be given in Chapter V, but in his "Greetings to the Fifteen Patriots" [73] (prisoners freed by the Government of Brazil in exchange for the release of Elbrick), Marighella asserted that the people

---

[70] *Ibid.,* p. 47.
[71] *Ibid.,* p. 48.
[72] *Ibid.,* p. 44.
[73] "Greetings to the Fifteen Patriots" in Ferreira, *op. cit.,* pp. 82-86.

of Brazil had approved of the kidnapping and that it had achieved its objective to obtain the release of the prisoners.

Moreover, he maintained that the Brazilian Government had been compelled to comply with "all" of the demands made by the revolutionaries—not only the release of the designated prisoners, but the publication of their revolutionary manifesto. Thus, the mass media which had been subject to strict governmental censorship were opened up for the first time since 1964. In addition, Marighella argued, the United States Government had also been humiliated and forced to issue a "direct order" to the junta urging it to accept the guerillas' terms. Referring to the fact that several different ideological tendencies were represented among the fifteen prisoners, Marighella repeatedly stressed that by their action the A.L.N. guerillas had attempted to show their basic unity on 1) the overthrow of the Brazilian military dictatorship and 2) the expulsion of U.S. influence from Brazil. In his view, the revolutionary war to accomplish these tasks was already underway in Brazil and the Elbrick kidnapping and its aftermath were only another episode in that war.

Another contribution of Carlos Marighella to the strategy of the urban guerilla was his concern for winning popular support and his suggestions regarding how to do so. Unlike Regis Debray, who tended to ignore this problem, Marighella emphasized the importance of public support for the guerillas and insisted that the best way to insure it was to persist in intervening in public issues and to continue to pursue the rebellion itself. He argued that as soon as a reasonable section of the population begins to take the urban guerillas and their action seriously, success is guaranteed. The government is forced to retaliate, to intensify repression, and to embark on "massive political persecution." Despite the initiation of police terror and the mobilization and use of the armed forces for police functions, the government will not be able to halt the scattered guerilla operations. In reaction to governmental repression, he continued, the populace will gradually refuse to collaborate with the authorities and turn instead to the revolutionary movement. Marighella concludes that "The role of the urban guerrilla, in order to win the support of the people, is to continue fighting, keeping in mind the interests of the masses and heightening the disastrous situation in which the government must act." [74] In a situation of such uncontrollable urban rebellion, rural guerilla warfare may then begin.

[74] Marighella, *Minimanual*, p. 54.

Whether or not Marighella's thesis of urban guerilla warfare expanding into the countryside will ultimately be proved or disproved in the cauldron of Latin American revolution, his depiction of governmental policies enunciated and actions taken in response to urban terrorism has in fact been largely substantiated in practice. In Brazil itself the activities of the A.L.N. have been met by increasingly repressive measures by the government in power. In Guatemala, the F.A.R. diplonapping of Ambassador von Spreti provoked a general "declaration of war" against the rebels—the Guatemalan Government proclaimed a national state of emergency, declared martial law, and instituted a house to house search of the capitol by armed patrols. The Government of Uruguay conducted a nationwide search for the kidnappers of Dan Mitrione and arrested over 100 persons for questioning; the President described the situation as "the greatest attack this country's political institutions have faced in this century." [75] In Canada as well, the terrorist tactics of the F.L.Q. which culminated in the murder of Quebec's Labor Minister, Pierre Laporte, provoked both a public Proclamation by Prime Minister Trudeau that Canada was threatened with insurrection, and the invocation of the War Measures Act in retaliation.

Before concluding this section on the role of urban terrorism within revolutionary strategies, a brief examination should be made of another major theme of contemporary revolutionary literature which depicts guerilla warfare in any one country as only part of an international revolutionary movement against capitalism in general and the United States in particular. This theme has had its theoretical and practical counterpoint not only in the writings and actions of Marighella, but also in the works and speeches of Castro, Ché and Regis Debray. It constitutes a common denominator of such otherwise nationally divided guerillas in Argentina, Bolivia, Brazil, Chile, Colombia, the Dominican Republic, Ecuador, Guatemala, Peru, Venezuela, and Uruguay—throughout Latin America. Equating United States involvements in Latin America with American imperialism, one critic of U.S. policies in Latin America has argued that in these countries a new attitude toward U.S. intervention is gradually evolving: "That attitude recognizes that the United States cannot be militarily defeated in one isolated country at a time. The U.S. cannot, on the other hand, sustain two, three, five Vietnams

[75] Quoted in the *New York Times,* August 11, 1970.

simultaneously. If it tried to do so, its internal economy would crumble." [76]
This anti-North American attitude of the Latin American revolutionary
is based not only on the long history of U.S. political and economic
involvements in Latin America or "domination" by the United States
in Latin American affairs, but also on the more recent U.S. policies of
anti-subversive warfare—including the provision of weapons and equipment and the training of military and police units.

The emphasis upon an international movement against capitalist society
may also be found in the writings of the Canadian F.L.Q., though the
anti-American overtones are less strident. Thus, Charles Gagnon, a
"leader-theoretician" of the Front, writes: "The strategic objective is
clear to everyone: It is the destruction of capitalist society and the
construction of an egalitarian society, . . ." [77] In Quebec, he argues, the
struggle for the overthrow of capitalism is inseparably linked to the
struggle for national independence. Moreover, "True independence is
inseparable from worldwide revolution and the fight goes on always and
everywhere, a fight to the death against imperialism, whether it be in
Vietnam or Guatemala." [78] This same spirit of international brotherhood
has been expressed by such diverse revolutionaries as Frantz Fanon,
Kwame Nkrumah, Ho Chi Minh, Mao Tse-tung, Fidel Castro, Carlos
Marighella and Stokely Carmichael.

Carmichael himself along with Eldridge Cleaver epitomizes the
internationally-minded revolutionary within the United States. Basically,
U.S. revolutionists may be grouped into three categories—the New Left,
the black radicals, and the student radicals. As Said and Collier have
pointed out in their book on *Revolutionism,* none of them has developed
an articulate revolutionist theory as a strategy for revolutionary action.[79]
Despite this lack of a theoretical framework (reminiscent of Debray),
the North American radicals do agree on the need for violence in order
to bring about basic political change. The use of violence is justified
by them: 1) as the only viable method available to them in order to
redress social ills, 2) as a method no different from the methods used
by the establishment to implement its own decisions, and 3) as the fastest

---

[76] Gerassi, John, "Part III: Introduction: Violence, Revolution and Structural
Change in Latin America" in Horowitz, de Castro, Gerassi (Eds.), *op. cit.,* p. 492.

[77] Quoted by Asselin, Gerard, "A Canada Divided" in *The Milwaukee Journal,*
November 11, 1970.

[78] *Ibid.*

[79] Said and Collier, *op. cit.,* pp. 96-97.

method available to destroy the system.[80] In the United States, violence has been used by minorities and other dissenting groups both as a threat and as a bargaining weapon in order to gain influence and power in a society in which they do not otherwise form part of the political bargaining process.[81]

As mentioned, the international outlook of the black revolutionary in the United States is well portrayed by Stokely Carmichael, particularly in his speech, "Black Power and the Third World," given at the 1967 conference of the Organization of Latin-American Solidarity. His own words best express the black power viewpoint: "We greet you as comrades because it becomes increasingly clear to us each day that we share with you a common struggle. We have a common enemy. Our enemy is white Western imperialist society. . . . Our struggle is to overthrow this system which feeds itself and expands itself through the economic and cultural exploitation of non-white, non-Western peoples—the THIRD WORLD."[82] Relating the black power movement within the United States to the revolutionary movements of Latin America, Carmichael observed: "Our people are a colony within the United States; you are colonies outside the United States. It is more than a figure of speech to say that the black communities in America are victims of white imperialism and colonial exploitation. This is in practical economic and political terms true." [83] Based on this parallelism of interests, he concludes that "Black Power means that we see ourselves as part of the Third World; that we see our struggle as closely related to liberation struggles around the world." [84]

The extremism voiced not only by Carmichael and Cleaver as spokesmen of the radical blacks, but also by student radicals such as the Weatherman faction of the SDS, has focused national attention on the growing phenomenon of violence in the United States and, as one of its manifestations, on political terrorism. As earlier sections of this chapter dealt with terrorism in Latin America, it may be helpful to outline briefly the concomitant appearance of political terrorism in the United States. A recent article on "Political Terrorism" has summarized the

[80] *Ibid.*, p. 26.

[81] Rose, Thomas (Ed.), *Violence in America,* p. 31. Random House, New York, 1969.

[82] Carmichael, Stokely, "Black Power and the Third World" in Ali, Tariq, *The New Revolutionaries,* p. 91. William Morrow & Co., Inc., New York, 1969.

[83] *Ibid.*, p. 95.

[84] *Ibid.*, pp. 101-102.

U.S. scene as follows: "A series of dynamite explosions in major cities, the discovery of makeshift bomb factories, police-sniping incidents and numerous acts of sabotage committed during campus disorders all have heightened fears that one or more dissident groups may be embarking on a campaign of terror. Suspicion falls mainly on white extremists of the New Left and ultra-militants in the Black Power movement. Terrorist action from the extreme right, however, is by no means absent from the scene." [85] After some attention to each of the above, the author specifically examined assassination and kidnapping as guerilla tactics clearly amenable to adaptation and use in the United States.

Supporting opinions for this conclusion were provided by the National Commission on the Causes and Prevention of Violence which reported in 1969 that the United States may be increasingly susceptible to an outbreak of political assassinations in the years ahead. Moreover, it has become quite apparent that governmental and congressional leaders are concerned that diplonapping à la Latin American style may be imported into the United States. The vulnerability of the United States to this kind of blackmail is heightened by its position as a host country not only to foreign diplomats in Washington, D.C., but to U.N. representatives, delegates, and personnel in New York City. Washington's uneasiness can be well understood when it is pointed out that "Police statistics show that members of foreign missions in New York and Washington were victims of 261 robberies, muggings and other assaults during the first six months of 1969." [86] With this record, they are hardly immune to the possibility of assassination or kidnapping.

In dealing with incipient revolutionaries and their terrorist activities, the United States Government has been torn between the need to preserve at least a minimum of law and order on the one hand and the equally valid need to allow nonviolent dissent and peaceful change on the other. As in the case of Trudeau's Canada, over-reaction could easily provoke greater resentment, increased violence, and wider support for the rebels among the "silent majority." Among the radical blacks and students, the Black Panthers and the SDS Weatherman faction have been singled out as extremists who are openly committed to revolutionary change—by violence, sabotage, and terrorism if necessary. Under the Nixon administration, federal action has been taken to increase and

[85] Shaffer, Helen B., "Political Terrorism" in *Editorial Research Reports — Volume I*, p. 341. Congressional Quarterly, Inc., Washington, D.C., 1970.
[86] *Ibid.*, p. 352.

improve surveillance of such radical groups, to increase the security guard of the White House and foreign embassies and legations in Washington, and to submit a legislative proposal for control of the sale of explosives.[87] Other measures will be discussed in Chapter VIII.

To conclude from this brief analysis of urban terrorism as a technique of revolutionary guerilla warfare, that terrorism has become the key to revolutionary progress and ultimate success would be both foolhardy and premature—and probably inaccurate. To maintain, however, that urban terrorism has been increasingly resorted to, used, and advocated by revolutionaries is simply a recognition of reality. Its shortcomings have been justly criticized as a technique which invites governmental reprisals and repression and may, in fact, alienate the very population needed for mass support. More seriously, the relevant political question is whether urban guerilla warfare, and the terrorism which it fosters, can ever lead to the acquisition of political power without which no objectives, no changes, no policies, and no programs can be achieved. If terrorism is to be regarded as a tactic of revolutionary strategy, will it lead to ultimate success or failure?

It is within this context that the diplomatic kidnappings must be examined. These are not merely isolated diplomatic incidents that have emerged as of passing interest to scholars and professors of international law. Nor are they purely national political problems which can be dealt with and solved within the confines of the foreign offices of individual sovereign states. The diplomatic kidnappings strike at the very foundations of international diplomacy and intercourse and as such they have burgeoned into a serious and complex problem of international concern. With the increase of revolutionary aspirations and activities within domestic as well as international life, the roots of violence have found a fertile ground, and assassinations and kidnappings have been spawned as their offspring. Both national and international efforts will be necessary to control their growth, but it will take eradication of the actual causes of revolution to ultimately sterilize the soil in which they flourish.

[87] *Ibid.,* p. 343.

CHAPTER II

THE DIPLOMAT AS VICTIM:
DIPLOMATIC INVIOLABILITY

Although diplonapping as a specific terrorist technique appears to be a relatively new phenomenon, its effectiveness is based on some very old and very simple realities: essentially, that if there are to be international relations between sovereign states they have to be carried on through some sort of regularized political intercourse or "diplomacy." In turn, if diplomacy is to be more than an abstract model of inter-state negotiations, it has to be conducted by men. These men have come to be called diplomats. To ensure the continuity of diplomatic contacts between themselves, states early recognized that their diplomatic agents would have to be secure both in their persons and in their residences. Hence, the concept of diplomatic privileges and immunities developed in tandem with the growth of diplomacy itself.

Formal representatives, whether envoys or ambassadors, have been exchanged between states as far back as ancient India and, in the Western world, early Greece. Although permanent missions were not utilized and the ambassadors were not professional diplomats in the modern sense of the term, their ability to represent their state and to defend its interests was paramount in their selection. Within the Amphictyonic League of the early Greek city-states, for example, orators and actors were often chosen for *ad hoc* diplomatic missions because of their persuasiveness in oratory.

Diplomatic privileges and immunities gradually developed as adjunct necessities to the early recognized principle of the personal inviolability of diplomatic agents. Thus, among the Greek cities,

Both heralds, the earliest kind of envoy, and ambassadors of all varieties were universally regarded as inviolable. The instances of breach of the rule were rare and seem always to have been followed by terrible reprisals . . .[1]

[1] Young, Eileen, "The Development of the Law of Diplomatic Relations" in *The British Year Book of International Law* (1964), p. 141. Oxford University Press, 1966.

Equally true in ancient India, diplomatic personages were considered inviolable and the receiving states were expected to make security arrangements for them.[2]

Although this early inviolability was based more on religious precepts than on legal rights, the international law of custom [3] and municipal law in code and practice soon provided a legal basis for it. Roman law regarded ambassadors as the personification of the sovereignty of the states they represented and therefore considered any offense against the person of an ambassador as an offense against his state. According to general custom, the aggrieved state could demand that any person who infringed upon an ambassador's inviolability should be surrendered to it; failure to make such "reparations" could lead to war. Even among the European tribes in the period following the fall of Rome,[4] diplomatic privileges were respected and penalties were imposed upon those harming envoys in transit, with special penalties for the murder of ambassadors.

It is not within the scope of this study to provide a detailed account of the growth of diplomatic relations from these early developments up to the 20th Century.[5] Rather, it will suffice to attempt to elicit from this period certain general practices and principles which emerged in relation to diplomatic privileges and immunities, particularly that of inviolability. With the vast expansion of trade and commerce in the 16th Century, for example, diplomatic contacts were also multiplied and with their increase came a concomitant change in diplomatic methods and characteristics.

As monarchs of different religious faiths (not only the Catholics and Protestants of Europe, but also the Muslim leaders of the Middle East, North Africa, and the Iberian peninsula) exchanged envoys, these representatives frequently had to be protected against local religious fanatics

---

[2] Chatterjee, H. L., *International Law and Inter-State Relations in Ancient India*, p. 66. Calcutta, 1958.

[3] Although the principle of diplomatic inviolability was recognized at this stage, the further development and expansion of the international law of diplomatic relations did not emerge in any great detail until the end of the 17th Century. Even then the treatment of diplomats was dependent largely on customary or municipal law and not on explicit treaties. See Young, *op. cit.*, p. 157.

[4] Salic law and the codes of the Alimani, Saxons, Frisians, and Lombards. Déak, F., "Classification, Immunities and Privileges of Diplomatic Agents" in *I Southern California Law Review* (1928), Vol. 209, pp. 213-214.

[5] For such an account, see Young, *op. cit.*, or Nicolson, Harold, *The Evolution of Diplomatic Method*, Constable & Co., Ltd., London, 1954.

and mob violence.[6] As a result, more detailed delineation of privileges and more elaborate procedures of protection were developed. Many of these have since withered away as, with more effective governmental protection, the necessity for them has declined. It is of particular interest to note that it is exactly in those areas today (i.e., Latin America, the Middle East, etc.) in which governments have not always been able to exert effective national controls to establish and maintain public order that the greatest number of cases of diplomatic kidnappings and/or violence against envoys has taken place. An initial parallel (which will be examined in Chapter VIII in greater detail) might imply that a step toward greater control could be the re-institution of more extensive rules of inviolability, procedures for protection, and penalties for violation.

By the 17th Century, the Venetian practice of sending resident ambassadors abroad had spread not only to the other Italian city-states but to all of Western and Central Europe. With the conclusion of the Treaty of Westphalia in 1648 and the subsequent establishment of modern nation-states with their legal attributes of political independence and sovereign equality, the modern system of international relations gradually emerged. That system necessitated regularized diplomatic contacts and new rules and regulations to govern them. In 1815 the Congress of Vienna specifically recognized that need by the adoption of a detailed classification of diplomatic agents for purposes of rank, precedence, and privileges. Many of these classifications have prevailed as accepted guidelines to diplomatic practice even up to the present time.

As the personal inviolability of diplomats became accepted in practice as a legal principle of customary international law, the theoretical rationale for it was also amplified. In addition to the fact that ambassadors were considered to be the personal representatives of their sovereigns and so to embody the dignity of their states, other theories for their inviolability were also raised. The now partially discredited concept of extraterritoriality—that diplomats (and others protected by special treaties) should be regarded as theoretically outside the territory of the recipient states, as if residing in their own countries—was advanced as another reason for diplomatic privileges and immunities and for the princ-iple of inviolability. With reference solely to diplomatic agents, the term basically denotes that they are not subject to the authority or jurisdiction

---

[6] Young, *op. cit.*, p. 146.

of the states to which they are accredited.[7] This is a notable exception to the sovereign jurisdiction of all states over all persons within their territory.

The final and perhaps most important basis for the inviolability of diplomats abroad arises from necessity itself. That is, international diplomacy is vitally dependent (though with the development of modern communications not totally so) upon the assured security of the diplomatic agents who conduct it. As early an authority as Grotius states:

Almost every page of history offers some remark on the inviolable rights of ambassadors, and the security of their persons, a security sanctioned by every clause and precept of human and revealed law. Nor is it surprising that the persons of those should be deemed inviolable, who form the principal link in that chain, by which sovereigns and independent states maintain their intercourse with each other.[8]

Or, phrased another way:

The privilege of a public minister is to have his person sacred and free from arrests, not on his own account, but on the account of those he represents, and this arises from the *necessity* of the thing, that nations may have intercourse with one another in the same manner as private persons, by agents when they cannot meet themselves.[9]

Further support for this rationale came from the Committee of Experts appointed by the League of Nations Assembly in 1926. Despite the Committee's decision that the whole question of diplomatic privileges and immunities was suitable for treaty regulation, that topic was not ultimately selected for action by the Hague Conference of 1930. The Committee nonetheless stated that in its opinion,

... the one solid basis for dealing with the subject is the necessity of permitting free and unhampered exercice of the diplomatic function and of maintaining the dignity of the diplomatic representative and the State which he represents ...[10]

Diplomatic privileges and immunities usually refer to freedom of communication and exemption from local jurisdiction as well as personal

---

[7] Satow, Sir Ernest, *A Guide to Diplomatic Practice* (4th Edition), p. 175. Longmans, Green & Co., London, 1957.

[8] Grotius, *The Rights of War and Peace*, p. 202. (Translated by A.C. Campbell, A.M.) Mr. Walter Dunne, Washington & London, 1901.

[9] Lord Chancellor Talbot in *Barbuit's* Case. Cited in Hudson, Manley O., Ed., *Cases and Other Materials on International Law*, p. 875. West Publishing Company, St. Paul, Minnesota, 1929. (Italics added.)

[10] *American Journal of International Law—Special Supplement* (July, 1926), Vol. 20, pp. 149-151.

inviolability; it is the latter principle, however, which is of most relevance to the problem of diplonapping. It is quite clear that the "inviolability" of diplomats implies more extensive privileges and greater protection than those provided for private individuals.[11] Although early writers differed on the extent of the personal privileges and immunities of ambassadors, even at the time of Grotius they agreed that *at least* these privileges included protection from unjust violence and illegal constraint.[12] Grotius himself argued, however, that the law of nations provided for a "greater extension of privileges," for if ambassadors were protected against nothing more than violence and illegal constraint, their so-called "privileges" would in fact confer no special advantage. Therefore, he stated, ambassadors are protected from *all* personal constraint and violence and all states are bound to respect these exemptions.[13]

This latter interpretation prevailed in practice and was subsequently codified first in municipal law; more recently it has been elaborated in international conventions. That codification did not take place in municipal law, however, until the end of the 17th Century when a number of diplomatic incidents impressed governments with the need to state, clarify, and/or implement what had already come to be accepted as customary international law. Thus, in 1679 the States-General of the Netherlands adopted a decree which forbad any arrest or execution of ambassadors for debts and in 1708 the British Parliament passed its own Diplomatic Privileges Act.[14] (Although domestic laws concerning the punishment of offenses committed by government agents or by private individuals against diplomatic agents are closely related to the laws defining diplomatic privileges and immunities, they are equally relevant to the question of state responsibility for the protection and security of diplomats and other aliens and will therefore be examined in Chapter III.)

---

[11] See Satow, *op. cit.,* p. 176. See also Plischke, Elmer, *International Relations: Basic Documents,* p. 12. D. Van Nostrand Co., Inc., Princeton, N.J., 1962.

[12] See Grotius, *op. cit.,* pp. 205-206.

[13] *Ibid.,* pp. 207, 209.

[14] The latter was proposed in pursuance to an incident in which the Russian Ambassador had been violently removed from his coach by "turbulent and disorderly persons," arrested to enforce payment of debts, and detained in custody for several hours. Although a trial found the accused guilty of the alleged acts, since these were not an offense at common law the courts had no power of punishment. The Diplomatic Privileges Act was an attempt to fill that particular gap in British domestic law. See Young, *op. cit.,* p. 158. Also cited in Satow, *op. cit.,* p. 177.

The international codification by treaty of the customary laws of diplomatic privileges and immunities took place even more recently than their domestic codification, although the municipal laws which existed admittedly lacked precision, detail, and uniformity as between different states. The first multilateral treaties dealing with the subject were the Convention on Diplomatic Officers and the Convention on Consular Agents, both adopted by the Sixth Inter-American Conference and signed at Havana, Cuba, 1928.[15] In summary, the former specified that all diplomatic officers, whatever their category, were entitled to the same rights, prerogatives, and immunities (Article 3) and that all diplomatic officers should be inviolable as to their persons, residence (private or official), and property, such inviolability covering all classes of diplomatic officers, the entire official personnel of the diplomatic mission, the members of their respective families, and the official papers, archives and correspondence of the mission (Article 14). Although the Convention on Consular Agents did not provide for the same privileges and immunities as those accorded to diplomats, it did specify that in the absence of any special agreements, consular agents could be neither arrested nor prosecuted, except when accused of committing a crime so designated by local legislation (Article 14).

The most recent—and most widely applicable—of the international agreements dealing with diplomatic privileges and immunities is the Vienna Convention on Diplomatic Relations adopted at the conclusion of the U.N. Conference on Diplomatic Intercourse and Immunities held in Vienna, March 2-April 14, 1961.[16] Drafted by the International Law Commission of the United Nations in 1958 (and greatly influenced by a 1932 Draft Convention on Diplomatic Privileges and Immunities written by the Harvard Law School Research in International Law), the Vienna Convention was discussed by 81 states participating in the conference which submitted over 350 amendments to it. The Convention entered into force April 24, 1964, with 63 signatures and 40 governments party to it.

---

[15] Printed in their entirety in *League of Nations Treaty Series*. Vol. CLV (1934-1935), Nos. 3581 and 3582. Although the United States is not a party to the Convention on Diplomatic Officers, it is a party to the Convention on Consular Agents.

[16] U.N. Doc. A/CONF. 20/13, April 16, 1961. Also found in 55 *A.J.I.L.* (1961) and in Plischke, Elmer, *op. cit.,* p. 22. Though signed by the United States, it had not been ratified at the date of writing; Senatorial advice and consent to ratification had been given, however.

Although it provides for the inviolability of the premises of the diplomatic mission (Article 22), of the private residence of diplomatic agents (Article 30), and of the archives, documents and official correspondence of the mission (Articles 24 and 27), as well as for the usual immunity of diplomatic agents both from the criminal jurisdiction of the receiving state and from its civil and administrative jurisdiction, with specified exceptions (Article 31), the Convention has most relevance for our purposes in its definition and protection of personal inviolability. Article 29 states:

The person of a diplomatic agent shall be inviolable. He shall not be liable to any form of arrest or detention. The receiving state shall treat him with due respect and shall take all appropriate steps to prevent any attack on his person, freedom or dignity.

The specific injunction that the receiving state "shall take all appropriate steps to prevent any attack on his person, freedom or dignity" bears directly on the matter of the diplonappings and will be discussed in greater detail in Chapters III and VIII.

Because of the importance of the Vienna Convention for the codification of the international law of diplomatic privileges and immunities, it is somewhat disconcerting that the United States had not ratified it by the end of 1972. Although there would have been no need for the House of Representatives even to consider the treaty, the Department of State submitted it both to the Senate and to the House along with the Diplomatic Relations Act of 1967, which was designed to complement it. In the hearing on the Convention itself before the Foreign Relations Committee of the Senate,[17] the State Department legal adviser justified the request for ratification on the grounds that the Convention would greatly clarify "the obligation of states concerning the treatment to be accorded foreign diplomatic missions and their personnel." Though mainly serving to codify principles already observed by governments in practice, the Convention would specify in detail exactly which privileges and immunities should be provided to different classes of diplomats. The Convention was subsequently sent to the floor of the Senate which gave its "advice and consent" to ratification on September 14, 1965.

---

[17] Vienna Convention on Diplomatic Relations: Hearing before the Subcommittee of the Committee on Foreign Relations, United States Senate (89th Congress - 1st Session) on Executive H, 88th Congress, 1st Session (July 6, 1965).

The Convention has not actually been ratified by the President, however, because of the failure of the House to pass the complementary legislation—the Diplomatic Relations Act of 1967. The State Department insisted on a sort of "package deal" by not depositing the United States ratification of the Vienna Convention with the United Nations until the related Act had also been passed. In his letter to the President of the Senate, then Secretary of State Dean Rusk wrote that the Diplomatic Relations Act would: allow certain privileges and immunities specified in the Vienna Convention to be accorded to diplomatic missions of non-signatory states, provide for more favorable treatment than that specified in the treaty to be accorded to certain foreign diplomatic missions depending on reciprocity, clarify the status in the United States of foreign heads of state and government and special envoys and specify their privileges and immunities, and repeal certain statutes whose terminology had become archaic and was inconsistent with the Vienna Convention.

In the hearings on the Act before the Senate Committee on Foreign Relations, the same purposes were emphasized.[18] Specifically, it was pointed out that the Act was designed to overcome certain inconsistencies which would arise if the Vienna Convention went into effect without complementary legislation. For example, although the Convention provides for privileges and immunities for members of permanent diplomatic missions, it does not apply to heads of foreign states or governments or to foreign ministers; the Diplomatic Relations Act would remedy this. It was argued that the customary privileges and immunities accorded to visiting heads of state or government should have some clear basis in the statutory law of the United States. The provision allowing for the extension of the privileges and immunities of the Vienna Convention to non-signatories on the basis of reciprocity was designed largely for purposes of uniformity, while the provision for more favorable treatment for certain missions than that specified in the Convention was included to allow the continuation of current U.S. practices with regard to exemption from federal taxes and immunity from civil and criminal jurisdiction for members of the administrative, technical and service staffs of various missions. The extension of diplomatic privileges and immunities to members of special diplomatic missions would be

---

[18] Diplomatic Relations Act of 1967: Hearing before the Committee on Foreign Relations, United States Senate (90th Congress - 1st Session) on S. 1577 to complement the Vienna Convention on Diplomatic Relations (May 9, 1967).

determined by the authority of the President. Although the Diplomatic Relations Act was passed by the Senate in June, 1967, and sent to the House where it was referred to the Foreign Affairs Committee, it had not been passed by the House as of date of writing.

The Vienna Convention on Consular Relations, drafted in Vienna in April, 1963,[19] may be considered as a companion document to the Convention on Diplomatic Relations and provides for similar, but not as extensive, privileges and immunities for consular officers. For example, although Article 10 provides for the inviolability of the archives, official documents and papers, and official correspondence in a consulate, Article 8 places certain exceptions on the total inviolability of the consular premises themselves and specifically states that they may not be used to afford asylum to fugitives from justice. Nonetheless, consular officers are not liable to arrest or detention pending trial, "except in the case of a grave crime and pursuant to a decision by the competent judicial authority" (Article 41-1) and they are furthermore not liable to the jurisdiction of the judicial or administrative authorities of the receiving state "in respect of acts performed in the exercise of consular functions" (Article 43). Finally, with regard to their own protection, the Convention does not blanket them with the total personal inviolability of diplomatic agents, but it does state that "The receiving State shall treat consular officers with due respect and shall take all appropriate steps to prevent any attack on their person, freedom or dignity." (Article 40).

Together, these two conventions on diplomatic and consular relations fairly extensively codify the international customary law on diplomatic privileges and immunities which had developed, as we have seen, from the very dawn of diplomatic relations. Although, as some writers have pointed out,[20] it is quite likely that different states will interpret various articles of the conventions according to their own historical traditions and their own municipal statutes, nevertheless the treaties provide an international statutory norm for the conduct of states in practice and perhaps a new guideline for future developments. By any measure they have certainly raised the codification, if not the actual protection, of the

---

[19] *Treaties and Other International Acts Series* (6820). Also in Department of State, Press Release No. 91, Feb. 16, 1949. This convention was ratified by the United States November 12, 1969, and entered into force for the United States on December 24, 1969.

[20]See particularly Young, *op. cit.,* pp. 180-182.

personal inviolability of diplomats to a new level of international legal validity.

A final document which deserves mention in this context is the Convention on the Privileges and Immunities of the United Nations.[21] Article IV deals with the privileges and immunities of the official representatives to the U.N. of member states. In Section II, *inter alia*, it provides for their immunity from personal arrest or detention and from legal processes, for the inviolability of their papers and documents, and for such other privileges, immunities, and facilities as other diplomatic envoys enjoy. Because of the vast expansion of the number of member states and the consequent blooming of national missions to U.N. headquarters in New York, the need for a general understanding regarding their diplomatic standing was clearly imperative. In addition to the national representatives themselves, the Secretary-General and all Assistant Secretaries-General are accorded the same privileges and immunities as other diplomatic envoys and the Secretary-General may also specify additional categories which then become eligible for such treatment (Article V, Sections 17, 18, 19). Though the U.S. did not accede to the Convention until April 29th, 1970, it has applied the provisions of the International Organizations Immunities Act (December 29, 1945) which contains similar, though not as extensive, privileges and immunities.[22]

According to both customary and codified international law, diplomats are legally entitled to their rights of inviolability, along with other privileges and immunities, as soon as they enter the territory of the receiving state, provided previous notification of appointment and arrival has been duly made to its government and accepted by it. Without prior notification, the mere production of formal credentials will suffice. Diplomats retain their diplomatic status throughout their official stay or tour of duty; nor is that status terminated by a state of war between their own country and that to which they are accredited. In such cases, in fact, the government of the receiving state is under a special obligation to protect them against either insult or injury and to ensure the security of their departure from the country.[23]

[21] *The American Journal of International Law: Official Documents.* Supplement, Vol. 43, 1949.

[22] Goodrich, Leland M., Hambro, Edvard, and Simons, Anne Patricia, *Charter of the United Nations* (3rd and Revised Edition), p. 625. Columbia University Press, New York & London, 1969.

[23] See Satow, *op. cit.,* p. 179.

Although Chapters V, VI and VII will deal with the specifics of the kidnappings themselves and Chapter VIII will attempt to analyze their legal and political implications, certain generalizations may be formed at this stage regarding diplomatic privileges and immunities as they relate to the recent diplonappings. We have seen that the personal inviolability of ambassadors and envoys was generally respected in practice and accepted as a principle of customary international law since the time of the early Greek city-states. Gradually, that principle became codified, first in municipal law in the 17th and 18th Centuries and more recently in international treaties and conventions. It has also been established that the inviolability of diplomats carries with it more extensive privileges and implies the necessity for greater protection than that afforded to private individuals or other aliens.

There appears to be no question whatsoever, then, but that the kidnapping of a foreign diplomat may be regarded not only as a violation of domestic law, but as a severe transgression of international law in terms of its general principles, established customs, and codified conventions. Diplonappings, regardless of the length of time of incarceration or the ultimate disposition of the diplomats themselves, present not only an infraction of such privileges and immunities as freedom of communication, but more seriously, infringe upon the personal inviolability of official state representatives. However, it should be pointed out that *state* responsibility for such infringements is not automatically incurred; rather, such responsibility is dependent upon direct or indirect state involvement in the violation of immunity or upon a case of clear negligence or lack of due diligence. This raises the question of exactly what responsibilities the receiving state incurs for preserving diplomatic inviolability; these state obligations for the protection and security of foreign diplomats will be examined in Chapter III.

CHAPTER III

PROBLEMS OF PROTECTION AND SECURITY

State responsibility for the protection of aliens—not to mention diplomats—arises both directly (through its own acts) and indirectly (through the acts of others). As in the fundamentalist view of sin, these acts may be considered as either positive, in the sense of acts of commission, or negative, as in acts of omission. Thus, Brierly maintains that "...a state incurs no responsibility for an injury suffered by an alien unless some fault either of commission or omission can be attributed to itself." [1]

As to a state's indirect responsibility, although a state is not automatically responsible for an injury against an alien inflicted by the act of a private individual, "Such an act, however, may be an occasion out of which state responsibility may *indirectly* arise, but only if it is accompanied by circumstances which can be regarded as in some way, *by complicity before or condonation after the event,* making the state itself a party to the injurious act of the individual." [2] In such cases it is necessary to ascertain whether the state was obligated to prevent the injurious act and whether it subsequently took the remedial steps required of it by its own laws. Under such an interpretation, responsibility is incurred when the injury would *not* have taken place if the state had been "reasonably diligent" (had exercised "due diligence") in its preventive actions.

There are obviously a number of subsidiary points which may be raised by this general topic of state responsibility.[3] First, in order to establish a *bona fide* case of direct responsibility, the action of com-

[1] Brierly, J. L., *The Law of Nations* (6th Ed.), p. 289. Oxford University Press, New York and Oxford, 1963. (Italics added.)
[2] *Ibid.*
[3] The following summary draws largely upon Amerasinghe, C. F., *State Responsibility for Injuries to Aliens.* Clarendon Press, Oxford, 1967. See particularly pp. 37-56.

mission or omission must be attributable to an official organ, agent, or representative of the state itself.[4] Clearly, as an abstract legal entity, the state can only act through individuals or groups of individuals and their official or unofficial character will largely determine whether or not the state is liable for their action. Secondly, the action must constitute a clear violation of an obligation established under international law.[5] In other words, the injury to the alien, whether or not considered as a breach of municipal law, must be designated as a breach of international law in order to incur state responsibility. Such violation, again, may arise from an act either of commission or of omission. A third criterion for the establishment of state responsibility requires that the act or omission must cause injury to the alien. Although such a requirement would appear to be self-evident, it might be useful to point out that the injury may consist of either material loss or moral suffering, although compensation for the latter has not consistently been awarded.

Detailed examination of direct state responsibility has less relevance to the diplomatic kidnappings, than an analysis of indirect responsibility. Suffice it to say, then, that *direct* responsibility (if the injuries and the violations meet the other criteria mentioned above) is incurred in practice only by acts committed or omitted by various authorities of the state itself. The specific state authorities which may invoke such direct responsibility by their acts or omissions include legislative bodies, administrative agencies, judicial organs, political subdivisions and/or successful insurgents. In contrast,

Acts or omissions of individuals, bodies, group(s) or organs which fall outside the above five categories ... are not as such imputed to the State. Responsibility of the State in connection with such acts or omissions will arise only as a result of *other*

---

[4] "States can only act by and through their agents and representatives." *P.C.I.J.* Series A/B No. 53, p. 91.

[5] There is abundant authority for this principle both in specific cases and in codification drafts. The Tribunal of the *International Fisheries Co. Case* stated, "States ... are responsible only for those injuries which are inflicted through an act which violates some principles of international law." *U.S.A. v. Mexico* (1931), 4 U.N.R.I.A.A., p. 701. See also the opinion of the General Claims Commission in the *Dickson Car Wheel Co. Case* in *U.S.A. v. Mexico* (1931), Opinions of Commissioners (1931), p. 187. Equally clearly, the 1926 Guerrero Report of the League of Nations Committee of Experts for the Progressive Codification of International Law stated, "A State is responsible for damage incurred by a foreigner attributable to an act contrary to international law or to the omission of an act which the State was bound under international law to perform." I.L.C. *Yearbook* (1956) ii, Annex I, p. 222.

acts or omissions of persons whose acts or omissions are actually imputable to the State...⁶

In these latter cases, state imputability can only arise if the damage suffered occurs because of an act or omission of the state itself, and not simply as a result of the original offense of private individuals.

With regard to offenses committed by private individuals, we have established that the state is not automatically responsible for their acts as such; rather, the acts of private individuals only *create* the occasion for the establishment of state responsibility (if in fact it fails either to prevent or to punish those acts, where possible, or positively encourages them). For example, if a violation of international law resulting in an injury to an alien occurs "as a result of the negligent omission of the State police to prevent it, then the omission of the State police may be attributable to the State..." and the state is therefore responsible.⁷ Nonetheless, a clear distinction should be maintained between the direct responsibility incurred by state agents, authorized and controlled by it and acting on its behalf, and private individuals. As Eagleton has pointed out, no state can be expected to exert "as vigorous a control" over the acts of private individuals as over the acts of its own agents.⁸

Despite this admitted limitation in practice on actual state control over individuals within their boundaries, states are obligated under international law to employ "due diligence" to prevent the commission on their territory of certain acts by private persons injurious to other states (for example, infringement upon the personal inviolability of a head of state or of his diplomatic representative). If prevention is not possible, punishment and reparations are required; state failure either to punish the offender or to provide proper court remedy for the injured alien results in state responsibility.⁹ Reparations may consist of disowning the act, expressing regret and/or apologies to the injured state, punishing the individual or individuals responsible, or paying compensation for any material damages. Such reparations arise not from the direct responsibility of the state but from its indirect responsibility—its

⁶ Amerasinghe, *op. cit.*, p. 54. (Italics added.)

⁷ *Ibid.*, p. 50.

⁸ Eagleton, Clyde, *The Responsibility of States in International Law*, p. 79. N.Y. University Press, New York, 1928.

⁹ See the *Janes Claim:* "The culprit is liable for having killed or murdered an American national; the government is liable for not having measured up to its duty of diligently prosecuting and properly punishing the offender." In *U.S.A. v. Mexico* (1926), 4 U.N.R.I.A.A., p. 87.

obligation to repair any material or moral damage caused by a violation of international law, even if that violation is not directly imputable to the state itself.[10]

States are therefore clearly obligated to provide both protection and reparations in cases of individual violations of international law resulting in injury to aliens. The degree of such protection and the amount of any reparations are far less clear. In terms of protection, although the state must furnish legislative, administrative, and judicial machinery that *normally* would protect the alien against injuries by private individuals, that machinery need not be so efficient as to prevent *all* injury to aliens.[11] More importantly, protection does imply that the state exercise "due diligence" to prevent the injury. However, the degree of local protection which must be afforded and the tests of state negligence in preventing private injury are uncertain questions indeed. Borchard maintains that in "normally well-ordered states" governmental liability is dependent upon its ability to protect the injured person in any given case. The particular circumstances of the case are paramount in determining state responsibility: "...if the moving cause of the injury is notorious, e.g. bandits in a certain locality, a greater degree of protection is incumbent upon the government than in cases of sudden violence which the best organized government could not foresee." [12] Thus, a prior demand for adequate police protection may provide a legal basis for reparations, if such protection is not subsequently provided and injuries are incurred.

Evidently, in less "well-ordered states" the rules of governmental liability were expanded in practice and interpreted more stringently to the detriment of the offending states. In the latter part of the 19th Century and in the early 20th Century, for example, governments of "more poorly organized countries like China, Turkey, Morocco and formerly Greece" were held liable for acts of private individuals even in the absence of

---

[10] Kelsen, Hans, *Principles of International Law* (2nd Edition), p. 199. Holt, Rinehart & Winston, Inc., 1966.

[11] Borchard, Edwin M., *The Diplomatic Protection of Citizens Abroad,* p. 213. The Banks Law Publishing Co., New York, 1915.

[12] *Ibid.,* p. 214. The test of state responsibility was also stated as the enforcement of its laws "with reasonable vigor and promptness, to prevent violence when practicable, or failing in that to punish the offenders criminally, and to indemnify the injured party by [its] remedial civil justice." Quoted in *ibid.,* pp. 214-215. Cited in *Mills (U.S.) v. Mexico* (July 4, 1868), Moore, John Bassett, *History and Digest of the International Arbitrations to Which The United States Has Been a Party (Vol. III),* p. 3034. Government Printing Office, Washington, D.C., 1898.

governmental complicity, "...presumably on the ground that an indifferent police protection and enforcement of the laws invited disorder and constituted in itself an international delinquency. In other words, liability is predicated on the *failure* to prevent the injury, regardless of *ability* to prevent it.[13] More recently, such unequal treatment (at one time even based on treaty obligations for "special protection" of all aliens) has come into nominal disrepute; however, the argument that liability may be incurred if the "norms" of adequate protection are not provided creates the necessity to distinguish between well-organized and poorly organized governments and implies differential treatment between them.[14] This bears particular relevance for the situation in Latin America today and will be examined in greater detail in Chapters V and VI.

As we have seen, the failure of any government to exercise due diligence in the prevention of private injury to aliens incurs indirect state responsibility. "The state is thus responsible for every injury which by the exercise of reasonable care it could have averted." [15] What constitutes "reasonable care" is, of course, open to argumentation. The United States has advanced the doctrine that the diligence required must be "commensurate with the emergency or with the magnitude of the results of negligence." [16] Eagleton quotes a more detailed but somewhat contradictory definition of due diligence as follows:

...the extent of the duties is to be commensurate with the extent of the means for performing the same, and ... he who has employed all the means within his reach has perfectly fulfilled his duty, irrespective of the material result of his efforts.[17]

In such an interpretation the *results* of preventive attempts, even if those attempts were ineffective, do not of themselves create negligence on the part of the state. This latter doctrine has generally been favored in Latin America as well as by many of the African and Asian states.

---

[13] *Ibid.,* p. 215.

[14] " ... the legal status granted to aliens must not remain below a certain minimum standard of civilization. The fact that the legal status granted to the citizens by the national law does not correspond to this standard is no excuse." See Kelsen, *op. cit.,* pp. 366-367. This interpretation of the requirements of protection is generally accepted in the United States and Europe; it is held in less repute in Latin American states which adhere to the "equality doctrine."

[15] Borchard, *op. cit.,* p. 217.

[16] *Ibid.,* p. 218. This has been disputed by some writers. See Hall, William E., *A Treatise on International Law* (6th Ed.), p. 217. Atlay, Oxford, 1909.

[17] Quoted in Eagleton, *op. cit.,* p. 89. Citation in the *Case of Salvador Prats,* Moore, *op. cit.,* p. 2894.

The test of whether or not due diligence has been exercised in fact is highly dependent upon the particular circumstances and whether they warrant "special protection." It has already been mentioned that in cases in which the danger is notorious or recurrent, extra efforts may be necessary to prevent anticipated injuries. Or, if a request has been made for protection or if prior warning has been given in time to take precautions, special diligence may be required. In general, if *any* special conditions exist calling for special notice, the diligence thereby required must be exercised accordingly. This special protection required by the doctrine of due diligence has particular relevance for the diplonappings in that most of the cases in question have involved dangers which were notorious and, after a time, recurrent; in many of them prior warnings had been given; and, in all cases, "special conditions" did exist. Moreover, even without such conditions, special protection is always required, without exception, in the case of official state representatives.

The special protection which governments are expected to afford to diplomats arises quite naturally from their diplomatic inviolability. It is recognized both as a general principle of international law and is also provided for in several municipal statutes. Moreover, injurious acts (attacks or insults) against diplomatic agents are regarded as injuries against the foreign state itself and any claim for redress is brought by that state in its own behalf. In support of his statement that special protection to diplomatic agents is well-known,[18] Eagleton cites the Corfu episode in which Italy regarded the murder of the Italian General Tellini as a direct insult to itself and subsequently collected heavy damages from Greece. The Committee of Jurists appointed by the Council of the League of Nations to consider responsibility in that case stated, "The recognized public character of the foreigner and circumstances in which he is present in its territory, entail upon the State a corresponding duty of special vigilance in his behalf." [19] An accurate summary of the

---

[18] *Ibid.,* p. 80. Or, again, he states that a special duty of protection is necessary for any foreigner of public character, pp. 91-92. See also Borchard, *op. cit.,* p. 216; Satow, *op. cit.,* pp. 176-177; and Sen, B., *A Diplomat's Handbook of International Law and Practice* (1965), p. 90. For *cases* which hold that the receiving state is under a clear obligation to afford "special protection" to foreign officials, see *U.S. v. United Mexican States* (Mallén), General Claims Commission (1927), Opinions of Commissioners (1927) and *U.S. (Chapman) v. Mexico,* General Claims Commission (1930), Opinions of Commissioners (1931).

[19] League of Nations, *Official Journal,* V, p. 524.

principle as attested to by most recognized authorities is given by Kelsen:

The head of a state, if he is staying on the territory of another state in time of peace and with the knowledge and consent of the government, and diplomatic envoys of a state received by another state must be afforded special protection by the other state. The protection consists in that the government concerned is obliged to prevent violations of their personal dignity, their personal safety, and their intercourse with their government at home; and if prevention proves to be impossible, to punish severely the delinquents. This is the so-called inviolability of heads of state and diplomatic envoys.[20]

In summary, special protection is accorded to diplomats as well as to heads of state and arises out of the principle of personal inviolability. As in the case of injuries to aliens in general, that inviolability may be infringed either by direct action of the state itself or by private individuals. The extent of special protection required varies according to the circumstances but, in addition to prevention, it normally requires prosecution for the offense as well as apology and redress. In *Respublica v. de Longchamps* (1784) the Court ruled that:

The person of a publc minister is sacred and inviolable. Whoever offers any violence to him, not only affronts the Sovereign he represents, but also hurts the common safety and well-being of nations: —he is guilty of a crime against the whole world.[21]

Moreover, as mentioned above, special municipal laws have also been enacted by most states to provide for the punishment of offenses committed by private individuals against diplomatic agents. In the United States, for example, the law provides that:

Whoever assaults, strikes, wounds, imprisons, or offers violence to the person of a head of foreign state or foreign government, foreign minister, ambassador or other public minister, in violation of the law of nations, shall be fined not more than $5,000, or imprisoned not more than three years, or both.
Whoever, in the commission of any such acts, uses a deadly or dangerous weapon, shall be fined not more than $10,000, or imprisoned not more than ten years, or both.[22]

If no specific municipal law exists, ordinary criminal law may be employed, provided the law specifies proper punishment and the trial is properly conducted.

---

[20] Kelsen, *op. cit.,* p. 366.

[21] *I Dallas,* pp. 111-118.

[22] *United States Code Annotated: Crimes and Criminal Procedure (#1-370),* Title 18, 112, p. 180 (R.S. 4062). West Publishing Co., 1969.

"Special protection," then, extends beyond prevention to the matter of punishment for violations of international law committed either by state agents or by private individuals. Such violations must be rectified by the receiving state through any reasonable means which will bring the offender(s) to justice; failure to do so gives rise to the right of reparation. Before the state of the injured party may initiate demands for such direct redress, however, local remedies must be exhausted. "An offending state should always be given the opportunity to punish individuals whose injurious actions it has not been able to foresee or prevent." [23] Direct diplomatic action arises only when such local remedies are absent, inadequate, or applied indifferently; for example, adequate basis for governmental liability is:

... the failure, after reasonable opportunity, to bring the offenders to justice. Incidental to this ground of liability is the inadequate punishment of guilty individuals, negligently permitting them to escape, or an inexcusable delay in investigating the facts. Closely related to these reasons for responsibility is a pardon or amnesty to offenders, by which the plaintiff is deprived of the right to try the question of liability, or the punishment of the guilty is avoided.[24]

An equally valid reason for direct state action to secure redress is denial of justice or denial of proper and adequate protection by the courts.

Direct state action in the sense of state demands for redress or reparations usually occurs in the case of ordinary aliens only if local remedies are not provided or inadequate, or if they have been exhausted without provision of satisfactory justice. In cases of violations of diplomatic inviolability in which there is evidence of lack of special protection (either failure of prevention or inadequate punishment) the injured diplomat's state may demand reparations for injury to itself through its official representative. In either situation, an international case exists which may provoke attempts to settle it by either amicable or non-amicable means, ranging from ordinary diplomatic negotiations at one end of the spectrum to the use of armed force or warfare at the other end. In between these two extremes the following methods may be utilized: good offices, diplomatic interposition, mediation, and arbitration (as amicable methods); and withdrawal of diplomatic representatives,

[23] Eagleton, op. cit., p. 82. Or, "... it is a generally recognized rule that the alien must exhaust any legal remedies available under the law ... before the state to which the alien belongs can make claims for reparation." Kelsen, op. cit., pp. 370-371.

[24] Borchard, op. cit., p. 218.

retorsion or retaliation in kind, display of force, and use of armed force (as non-amicable methods).[25]

A final word should perhaps be inserted as to factors which may *limit* state liability for injuries to aliens, particularly with respect to diplomats. For example, the question may be raised as to whether the diplomat's own conduct placed him in a situation in which injury was likely to occur or his safety likely to be impaired—such as unreasonably exposing himself to a disorderly crowd. Moreover, despite the recognition of diplomatic privileges and immunities, diplomats are generally expected to observe the laws of the host country. If they fail to do so, particularly in an open and flagrant manner, they may provoke hostile attitudes and perhaps even overt actions against themselves.

This question of ensuring the security of diplomats residing among a hostile populace raises the possibility of a "twilight zone" in which although state protection is obviously called for, the degree of protection necessary may be uncertain. The host country is clearly obligated to afford "adequate protection," including special precautionary measures such as the posting of police guards at the embassy or the provision of an armed escort for envoys. Yet in any volatile situation "adequate protection" becomes as vague a security term as "due diligence" has been seen to be in legal parlance. Such uncertainty is compounded in cases of political turmoil, mob actions, insurrections, and civil wars.

In situations in which mob injuries occur, state responsibility theoretically arises on the basis of the same criteria as those applied to acts by private individuals. Eagleton argues that "If a state uses the means at its disposal in a diligent manner for the prevention of injuries, and properly enforces its measures of redress, it can no more be held to responsibility for the acts of a mob than for those of single individuals." [26] Yet, he states elsewhere that in practice mob cases usually do involve the payment of damages, "since there is usually sufficient warning to allow the government to take unusual precautionary measures." [27] Furthermore, in the case of diplomats, their status entitles them to a special

---

[25] See *ibid.*, pp. 439-450. These will be referred to again in Chapters V, VI and VII in which the diplonapping incidents themselves are examined in detail. The *legal* use of armed force is, of course, limited by several treaties as well as by the United Nations Charter.

[26] Eagleton, *op. cit.*, p. 127.

[27] Eagleton, Clyde, *International Government* (3rd Edition), p. 127. The Ronald Press Co., New York, 1957. Nonetheless, if the situation is beyond the control of "usually adequate forces," the state cannot be held liable.

protection which has resulted usually in the prompt payment of any indemnities incurred even for attacks by mobs on foreign consuls or consular agents, such being considered injured not as individuals but as representatives of a foreign state.[28]

As to insurrections and civil wars, when a government is unable to prevent injurious acts by private individuals in conditions of civil commotion, it is not automatically responsible for injuries which may be received by aliens in the course of such struggles. Claims based on damages incurred by aliens in civil wars have seldom been prosecuted successfully, except in Latin America where the argument has been invoked that a state cannot avoid responsibility if it deliberately prefers anarchy. Thus, the test as to whether due diligence has been exerted in the attempted prevention of injuries arising from civil wars is based on the assumption "that the government is reasonably well-ordered, and that revolution and disorder are abnormal conditions." [29] Neither mobs nor civil wars as such, then, create a situation which of itself will incur state responsibility. Rather, riots and other civil disturbances are neither automatically exempt, nor is the state automatically responsible for injuries in such cases. Responsibility, once again, must be determined by the rules of due diligence and by the presence and effectiveness of local remedies and justice.

Brigandage—or kidnapping—does not fall far afield from the generalizations reached above. Unless the government has neglected to take adequate action in order to attempt to prevent the brigandage or to punish the guilty, the state is not liable. Moreover, Borchard states,

Question has often arisen as to the liability of the defendant states for ransoms demanded by and paid to brigands by claimants or their governments. The claimant state (i.e., the national state of the victim) has only in rare cases, as a matter of humanity, advanced the price of a ransom for payment to brigands. Reimbursement has on several occasions been demanded of the defendant state or else that state has been asked to make a direct payment to the brigands. Only in rare instances have such demands been successful, and then only because actual or implied complicity or negligence of the state was asserted or admitted.[30]

Finally, in cases of revolutionary activities by private persons against foreign states (only tangentially related to the diplonappings), no special protection of aliens is required of the state of residence. Rather, its sole

[28] Borchard, *op. cit.*, p. 223.
[29] *Ibid.*, p. 230.
[30] *Ibid.*, p. 220.

duty is to afford aliens with the same security from assassination which it affords to others resident in its territory.[31]

For purposes of summary, the indirect responsibility of a state for protection to aliens arises only when the state itself, through its agents, fails to prevent, punish, or remedy any violation of international law by private persons which results in injury to an alien. Moreover, the personal inviolability of diplomats, discussed in Chapter II, creates the additional obligation of "special protection" to be afforded to foreign envoys; such protection includes not only special vigilance to prevent injurious acts, but also prosecution, punishment, apology, and redress for injuries which it is unable to prevent. If such special protection is not provided and if adequate local remedies are lacking, the injured diplomat's state may demand reparations from the state of residence. Although mob actions, insurrections and civil wars often complicate the legal picture, the rules of due diligence in prevention and punishment through local remedies generally continue to apply.

The entire topic of state responsibility for the special protection of diplomatic agents, though an important perquisite of diplomatic inviolability, certainly does not exhaust the subject. For example, such matters as the arrest and/or detention of foreign representatives by state officials themselves and cases involving violations of diplomatic dignity directly impinge upon the personal inviolability of envoys and thus also involve state responsibility. Nonetheless, they are less relevant to the diplomatic kidnappings than cases of actual physical attack or personal injury by private individuals and hence will be mentioned only as they relate directly to such actions. A more extensive examination of the specific cases of assault and attack on diplomatic personages will be made in Chapters V-VII. Chapter IV will next analyze the rights—and the limitations—of political asylum.

[31] Lauterpacht, H., "Revolutionary Activities by Private Persons Against Foreign States" in 22 *A.J.I.L.* (1928), p. 127.

ASYLUM, EXTRADITION, AND THE POLITICAL OFFENSE

The problems created by the numerous cases of actual or attempted diplonappings have been compounded by the legal status of diplomatic asylum in Latin America. Although this book deals broadly with the diplomatic kidnappings in general, it is nonetheless recognized that the majority of the recent diplonappings have taken place in Latin America. Though some of them have been conducted for ransom, most were designed to secure a "trade" of certain political prisoners for the kidnapped diplomats. Temporary asylum for the freed prisoners within some foreign embassy has frequently been part of the bargain. This is particularly a problem in Latin America because it is precisely there where the concept of diplomatic asylum for political refugees has been most firmly established in practice, if not in law. Before reviewing such regional customs, however, a brief survey of the status of asylum in general international law may provide a better background for them.

"Asylum is the protection which a state grants on its territory or in some other place under the control of certain of its organs, to a person who comes to seek it." [1] It may be helpful to distinguish at the outset between territorial asylum granted within the territorial boundaries of a state and therefore within its political and legal jurisdiction, and extra-territorial asylum granted by embassies, legations and consulates within the territory of another state. There is no dispute over the legal right of a state to grant asylum within its own boundaries since control over entry and departure from its territory is a necessary corollary of its territorial sovereignty. Although international law clearly recognizes territorial asylum as a right of every state, it does not recognize it as a right of the individual concerned. "Thus, while the state has complete

---

[1] Article I, Resolution adopted by the Institute of International Law, September, 1950. Printed in *American Journal of International Law, Supplement,* Vol. 45 (1951), p. 15.

discretion to grant or to refuse asylum, there is no right of the individual to demand it." [2] It is usually granted on humanitarian grounds to political offenders or to fugitives from justice *unfairly* prosecuted.

Regarding the status of extra-territorial asylum at the present time, Satow states: "It is now an established doctrine in Europe that no *right* to give asylum to political refugees in the house of a diplomatic agent exists." [3] However, he does point out that the practice has been extensively followed in the past. This was particularly true of the 16th and 17th Centuries when the "right" of extra-territorial asylum was "almost invariably" accepted [4] as part and parcel of the inviolability of the embassy which, as we have seen, was well-established in custom. Thus, although the theorists generally agreed even then that ambassadors should *not* grant asylum to criminals, political or otherwise, the common practice was exactly the opposite: " ... the embassy could afford protection to all offenders except those who were suspect of high crimes against the state itself." [5] Extra-territorial asylum was allowed in practice, then, as an aspect of the principle of ambassadorial immunity and inviolability.

During the 19th Century, however, the concept of extra-territorial asylum as a right gradually faded from the scene of European international relations—both in law and in practice.[6] At present, most writers agree that the practice of extra-territorial asylum is neither based on nor sanctioned by international law and that " ... it can be defended only on the ground of the *consent* of the state within whose jurisdiction it is sought to be maintained." [7] Despite its dubious legal standing, such asylum has nonetheless been granted occasionally—particularly, as will be seen, in Latin America. Such practice, however, has been regarded as a regional exception to the general system of international law which prevails elsewhere.[8]

---

[2] García - Mora, Manuel R., *International Law and Asylum as a Human Right*, p. 3. Public Affairs Press, Washington, D.C., 1956.

[3] Satow, *op. cit.*, p. 219. (Italics added.)

[4] Adair, E. R., *The Exterritoriality of Ambassadors in the Sixteenth and Seventeenth Centuries*, p. 254. Longmans, Green and Co., New York, 1929.

[5] *Ibid.*, p. 225.

[6] Oppenheim, L., *International Law: A Treatise* (7th Ed., by H. Lauterpacht), p. 794. Longmans, Green and Co., New York, 1955.

[7] Moore, *A Digest of International Law*, II, p. 779. Government Printing Office, Washington, D.C., 1906. (Italics added.)

[8] Morgenstern, Felice, "Extra-territorial Asylum," p. 242. In *The British Yearbook of International Law* XXV (1948).

An accurate summary of the role of extra-territorial asylum in law and practice is given by C. Neale Ronning in his book on *Diplomatic Asylum:*

> The only generalization which seems at all acceptable is that the practice of states in this regard is not based upon any generally recognized *right of asylum* so far as general international law is concerned. Instead, it is a *de facto* result of the fact that international law accords to the various accredited diplomatic officers certain well-recognized immunities from local jurisdiction, such as immunity of their official residences and offices from invasion by local authorities. Humanitarian, political or other motives may lead to the original grant of asylum but once the refugee is inside the legation the territorial state is faced with an insoluble dilemma. Assuming the state of refuge will not surrender the refugee, the territorial state can apprehend him only by violating the immunity of the diplomatic premises or, possibly, by breaking diplomatic relations. The fact is that such extreme measures are considered too high a price to pay for apprehension of the refugee.[9]

As Ronning points out, however, the fact that there is no practical remedy for the territorial state in such a situation does not thereby establish asylum as a legal right possessed by the state of refuge. Rather, as stated above, it is an exception to the norm—an exception which is based more on the exigencies of expediency than on the rule of law.

Though an exception in general international law, extra-territorial asylum is nevertheless the common rule in Latin American practice. There it has been utilized primarily to protect political refugees; it has been justified on the grounds that in conditions of perennial political instability and revolutionary ferment, political asylum is a necessary and useful device to circumvent prosecutions for political offenses or arbitrary incarceration. Because of the ever-present possibility of political *coups,* current governmental leaders prefer to maintain an institution which (however annoying to them while in power) might someday benefit them.[10] There is abundant evidence of the prevailing custom of extra-territorial asylum in Latin American practice in the 20th Century. For example, a subcommittee of the Committee on International Public

---

[9] Ronning, C. Neale, *Diplomatic Asylum,* p. 22. Martinus Nijhoff, The Hague, 1965.

[10] According to Adair, "Obviously what we have here is a survival of seventeenth-century practice for a particular class of offenders and because of a peculiar condition of affairs: governments have been in the past so unstable in Latin America that even the victorious leader in a revolution will not press too hard on a refuge which for the moment is protecting his enemies, but which, by the next turn of fortune's wheel, may be invaluable as an asylum for himself." See Adair, *op. cit.,* p. 205.

Law reported at the Sixth International Conference of American States (Havana, 1928) [11] that a large majority of American states did not consider proper the application of strict or unbending rules to special asylum cases and that humane sentiments should be taken into consideration. Moreover, it stated that the practice of a majority of American nations could be invoked—"a practice which consecrates the right of asylum" as has been proved in "frequent" cases. Or, again, in response to the Bolivian revolution of 1946, the members of the diplomatic corps in Bolivia unanimously referred to the practice of asylum and safe-conduct for political refugees as "customary American law." This regional practice was also recognized by the Argentine government in 1937 in a note to its foreign diplomatic representatives which emphasized that "the continent of America is that in which the right of asylum has been respected in practice and codified expressly in international agreements." [12]

Whether or not such an established practice actually represents regional *law*, however, is quite a different matter. At the end of an entire chapter devoted to Latin American practice in this regard, Ronning summarizes that practice as follows:

In spite of eloquent statements proclaiming the virtues of the institution, there has been a reluctance on the part of a majority of the Latin American states to declare unequivocally that they regard the granting of diplomatic asylum to persons pursued for political acts as a *right* appertaining to the state of refuge and the respect of such asylum as a *duty* incumbent upon the territorial state in deference to *a custom recognized as law.* [13]

He argues that in fact Latin American governments permit, deny or discuss diplomatic asylum according to political contingencies, not legal considerations. Ronning concludes that both the general reluctance of Latin American states to claim or admit that the practice of diplomatic asylum is sanctioned by a rule of law and the statements asserting that it is *not* sanctioned by a rule of law make it impossible to say that such asylum is actually a custom having the force of law.

Because of this ambiguity regarding its legal standing, it could be argued that asylum is simply a political fact in Latin American life and should therefore be dealt with in political, not legal, terms. Thus, in approaching the problem of the diplonappings, a salutary move might

[11] International Conference of American States, Sixth (1928), *Minutes and Reports of the Committees,* Part I (Havana, 1928).
[12] Quoted in Ronning, *op. cit.,* p. 33.
[13] *Ibid.,* p. 94. (Italics added.)

be to attempt to achieve a general agreement among the Latin American states that asylum will not be granted to any political prisoners who are designated by the kidnappers to be traded for diplomats held as hostages. However, because asylum is so firmly established in practice, such agreement may be extremely difficult to achieve, particularly between those states who do regard the practice as sanctioned by regional law. Moreover, there are certain Latin American conventions and treaties providing for asylum which are binding on those states parties to them. At least two of these would have to be specifically modified to allow the *denial* of asylum in the special cases of diplonappings.

As early as 1889 a Treaty on International Penal Law provided for asylum in embassies or legations for persons pursued for political reasons, with the proviso that the chief of the mission was obligated to inform immediately the government of the territorial state about such a fact and that the government could demand that the refugee leave its territory within the shortest time possible. The mission head in turn could demand whatever guarantees might be necessary to allow the fugitive to leave the country without interference. This convention was only signed and ratified by five states, however.[14] A 1939 Treaty on Political Asylum and Refuge amplified the 1889 treaty and reconfirmed the right of asylum provided therein; it has been ratified, however, by only two states.[15] Of more significance for general contractual obligations are the Convention on Asylum (Havana, 1928), the Convention on Political Asylum (Montevideo, 1933), and the Convention on Diplomatic Asylum (Caracas, 1954) since all three were signed at international conferences attended by all of the American states.

The Havana Convention on Asylum [16] contains two provisions relevant to the subject matter of this Chapter. Article I, a limiting article, states that it is *not* permissible for states to grant asylum in legations to persons accused of or condemned for *common crimes*; if such persons have taken refuge in a legation they must be surrendered upon request to the local government. Article II, on the other hand, states that "Asylum

---

[14] These are: Argentine Republic, Bolivia, Paraguay, Peru, and Uruguay. See Ronning, *op. cit.,* p. 54. See also Satow, *op. cit.,* p. 221.

[15] These are Uruguay and Paraguay. Ronning, *op. cit.,* pp. 54-55.

[16] Reproduced in de Vries, Henry P., and Rodriguez-Novás, José, *The Law of the Americas,* pp. 269-270. Oceana Publications, Inc., Dobbs Ferry, N.Y., 1965. (Ratified by: Brazil, Colombia, Costa Rica, Cuba, Dominican Republic (denounced), Ecuador, El Salvador, Guatemala, Haiti, Honduras, Mexico, Nicaragua, Panama, Paraguay, Peru, Uruguay.)

granted to political offenders in legations ... shall be respected to the extent in which allowed, as a right or through humanitarian toleration, by the usages, the conventions or the laws of the country in which granted." In addition, the article provides that such asylum should be granted only in urgent cases and for the period of time necessary to ensure safety, that the fact must be immediately reported to the Foreign Minister of the territorial state, and that that government may request that the refugee leave the national territory in the shortest possible time. (This clear distinction in treatment between persons accused of common crimes and those accused of political crimes is universally recognized in law and practice; the practical problems of determining which is which in a particular case will be discussed below.)

The qualification in Article II that asylum shall be respected only to the extent allowed "by the usages, the conventions or the laws of the country in which granted" severely weakens the force of the treaty in terms of any generally accepted legal rule. The Colombian-Peruvian Asylum Case in which the treaty was invoked did little to clarify the status of asylum as generally accepted custom and, in fact, Ronning argues that "all parties were agreed that no general recognition of asylum had been established by the treaty" and later concludes that "the treaty was not intended to establish any general right of asylum even among the signatories—much less in 'Latin American International Law'." [17] The Convention on Political Asylum signed in Montevideo in 1933 and designed to "define" the terms of the Havana Convention is almost as ambiguous as the 1928 document and did not establish any generally accepted "right of asylum" any more than its predecessor did.

Most important in terms of actually establishing a "right" of asylum among its signatories is the Convention on Diplomatic Asylum signed at the Tenth Inter-American Conference held at Caracas in March, 1954.[18] Article I provides that asylum granted in legations to persons sought for political reasons or for political offenses should be respected by the territorial state in accordance with the provisions of the Convention. Article II states even more explicitly: "Every State has the right to grant asylum; but it is not obliged to do so or to state its reasons for refusing it." This particular provision, then, would obviously have to be revoked

[17] Ronning, *op. cit.,* pp. 57 and 61.
[18] Reproduced in de Vries and Rodriguez-Novás, *op. cit.,* pp. 273-277. Ratified by: Brazil, Costa Rica, Ecuador, El Salvador, Haiti, Mexico, Panama, Paraguay, Peru, Dominican Republic, Venezuela.

or modified if any agreement to *deny* asylum is to be reached as a means of inhibiting and limiting the diplomatic kidnappings. Finally, in Article IV the state granting the asylum is given the right to determine the nature of the offense of the refugee and the motives of the territorial state for his prosecution. As mentioned, it is in that determination that many of the practical problems of asylum arise.

In addition to the questions surrounding the political exercise of asylum as established in practice and the legal right of asylum as established in treaty, there are several related issues. One concerns the duty of a state granting asylum to surrender to local authorities those accused of common crimes and therefore the need for that state to decide if a particular offense is a political offense or a common crime. Under Article IV of the 1954 Caracas Convention the right to make that decision is unilaterally given to the state granting asylum but this is not binding on non-signatory states. Moreover, there are numerous cases in which that unilateral right has been challenged or in which the decision reached by the state of asylum has not been accepted as valid by the territorial state. When this occurs it provokes the further question as to whether the state granting asylum has the duty to secure a safe-conduct out of the country for the refugee and, if so, whether the territorial state has the obligation to provide such safe-conduct.

With regard to political offenses, Latin American practice provides no clear guidelines as to what may be considered as "political" offenses in contrast to common crimes. Exact charges are not always made explicit and, when given, are only provided in vague and uncertain terms. Ronning makes four generalizations on Latin American practice as follows: [19] 1) the cases themselves cannot be used to help define political offenses because the territorial states have not always made it clear when demanding a refugee whether their demand was based on the nature of the crime as nonpolitical or because the asylum granted should only afford temporary protection regardless of the nature of the charge, 2) states have generally granted asylum to members of overthrown governments regardless of the nature of the charges against them; in such cases the territorial state has often denied that the crimes charged were in fact political in nature, 3) individuals involved in revolutionary movements have been given asylum regardless of the charges against them, and 4) even when the refugee was given safe-conduct out of the country by the government of the territorial state

[19] Ronning, *op. cit.,* pp. 184-185.

there is no evidence that this was granted because of concurrence by both states either in the nature of the offense or in the conditions under which asylum was originally granted. Thus, Ronning concludes, Latin American practice simply shows that asylum has been granted when the diplomatic representative concerned "felt" that the refugee was pursued for political reasons and that such decision-making has been a "highly intuitive process" on his part; all of this, he maintains, simply emphasizes "the extra-legal character of the whole institution." [20]

In contrast to extra-territorial asylum, in cases of territorial asylum states possess "an almost unlimited competence" to grant or to deny asylum to those prosecuted for political offenses.[21] Although Article 14 of the Universal Declaration of Human Rights [22] states that "Everyone has the right to seek and to enjoy in other countries asylum from prosecution," the Declaration itself has no legal status and therefore is not legally binding. Rather, it is generally recognized that the granting of territorial asylum is a right possessed only by the state and that the actual exercise of that right is "permissive" and not obligatory. The state itself, then, determines whether or not it will grant or deny asylum to a political refugee in any particular case. Such determination is usually based on a mixture of humanitarian considerations and domestic and foreign policy imperatives.[23]

When a refugee requests territorial asylum because of persecution for a political offense, his plea may be presented as an argument in exclusion, expulsion or extradition proceedings.[24] Exclusion of aliens from the country prior to entry or expulsion from it after residence therein are matters of domestic legislation and are not subject to international law or treaties. With regard to any requests for territorial asylum for political prisoners who might be offered in "trade" for kidnapped diplomats, therefore, the state of requested asylum may unilaterally deny such asylum by excluding their entry in the first instance or by denying their continued asylum, after entry, by expulsion. Such unilateral declarations of intent might be resorted to as another method of discouraging the diplonappers by eliminating the sanctuary of terri-

---

[20] *Ibid.,* p. 186.

[21] García-Mora, *op. cit.,* p. 73.

[22] "Text of the Universal Declaration of Human Rights," *Yearbook on Human Rights for 1948,* p. 467. United Nations, Lake Success, N.Y., 1950.

[23] Evans, Alona E., "Reflections Upon the Political Offense in International Practice," p. 2. In 57 *A.J.I.L.* (1963).

[24] *Ibid.,* p. 4.

torial asylum for any political prisoners whose release has been requested in exchange demands.

Extradition, unlike exclusion or expulsion, is governed in international
law both by custom and by convention. As in decisions regarding
asylum itself, extradition is granted or denied depending largely on
whether or not the state of asylum regards the refugee as a political
offender. The state's exercise of its right of extradition is as much a
matter of discretion as its exercise of the right of asylum. The legal
right to *refuse* to extradite persons for political offenses in well-established
in the Latin American legal system, it is recognized in all bilateral
treaties between the United States and the Latin American republics
and in several international conventions, and it is included in the domestic
legislation of a majority of those Latin American states.[25] In practice
as well, states generally have refused to extradite fugitives when the
possibility exists that they will be persecuted for political reasons.
What then constitutes a political offense? This question lies at the heart
of the matter and, as we have seen in Latin American practice, it is not
easily answered.

Basically, the decision as to whether a particular crime is a political
offense or an act related to a political offense is made by the country
requested to extradite the fugitive. In arriving at that decision the state
of asylum has little in the way of clear definitions or criteria to guide it.
"Purely political offenses" have been defined as "acts against the
security of the state" [26] or as treason, sedition, or espionage.[27] Because
of the difficulty of defining "relative political offenses" (those connected to or affected by common crimes), some limitations on the
concept of the political offense have been developed in practice and in
law.[28] One of these is the so-called Belgian *attentat* clause which
specifies that attacks (by murder, assassination, or poisoning) on the head
of a state or on members of his family shall not be considered as
political crimes; this clause has been widely included in extradition

---

[25] de Vries and Rodriguez-Novás, *op. cit.,* p. 87. See Convention on Extradition
Adopted by the Seventh International Conference of American States (Montevideo,
1933). League of Nations Treaty Series, Vol. CLXV (1936), No. 3803. The 1971
O.A.S. Treaty which provides for extradition procedures for those charged or
convicted of diplomatic kidnapping will be examined in Chapter VIII.

[26] García-Mora, *op. cit.,* p. 76.

[27] Evans, *op. cit.,* p. 11.

[28] The following limitations on the political offense are discussed in García-Mora,
op. cit., pp. 82-93.

treaties. Anarchistic offenses constitute a second limitation upon political offenses in that they are not considered as such and can therefore give rise to the exercise of the right of extradition. A third and relatively new category of offenses not considered to be political offenses are acts of collaboration with the enemy in wartime. Although traitors have traditionally been regarded as political offenders, recent trends have been to call for their extradition in various treaty provisions; in the absence of such provisions, the asylum state may exercise its own discretion. A fourth limitation on political offenses are those acts which have been designated as war crimes or crimes against humanity; these too do not merit exclusion from extradition proceedings.

Neither extradition treaties nor domestic extradition statutes, though providing for the exception of political offenses, are very explicit in specifying what constitute such offenses. As seen above, political offenses may be qualified in a negative way, however, by *excluding* certain acts from that category. Although the League of Nations attempted to prevent and control acts of terrorism by a convention outlawing it and providing for its punishment by an international criminal court, these efforts never resulted in a ratified treaty. Diplomatic kidnapping has been considered to be a common crime under the O.A.S. Convention of 1971, however, and the Convention provides for extradition proceedings in such cases. Although extradition statutes do not usually define political offenses as such, criminal codes and statutes may classify such offenses; among such political offenses in statutes are included treason, rebellion, sedition, insurrection, sabotage, espionage, and various military offenses.[29]

In an examination of fifty actual extradition cases in which political offense was offered as a defense against extradition, the plea was rejected and extradition granted in those cases in which homicide was committed as an isolated act, as an act of terrorism, treachery, personal revenge or without political objective; the political offense plea also failed in a majority of cases of arson, bombing, or kidnapping.[30] Such cases illustrate what has been seen as a tendency toward restriction of the concept of the political offense—a restriction also seen in the texts of various extradition treaties, in League efforts to outlaw terrorism,

---

[29] Evans, *op. cit.*, pp. 16-17. Note, however, recent trends toward *excluding* "treason" from the category of political offenses.

[30] *Ibid.*, p. 18.

and in U.N. attempts to exclude war crimes from the category of political offenses.

Moreover,

Given present international conditions and the vulnerability of those states, which are afflicted by disturbed political conditions, inexperienced in popular government, or economically underdeveloped, to espionage, terrorism, fomentation of civil war, or acts of international aggression, a strong argument can be made for further restricting the scope of the political offense by excluding these acts from its purview.[31]

Such an argument assumes a particularly favorable aspect when regarded in the light of Latin American instability today and the diplonappings which are so dependent on it. It is quite clear, for example, that although the political prisoners involved in the kidnapping exchanges would not necessarily be affected by a contraction in the definition of the political offense, the diplonappers themselves would be. As acts of terrorism, the diplonappings cannot be considered as anything but common crimes whose perpetrators have no recourse to asylum and are thus subject to extradition.

Because of the obvious interest of the United States in this matter, it is necessary to summarize the U.S. position on diplomatic asylum before concluding this Chapter. As far as the granting of extra-territorial asylum in embassies and legations in the United States itself is concerned, the U.S. government has never recognized the right of diplomatic missions in its territory to grant asylum; moreover, the right to grant diplomatic asylum in the U.S. has never been claimed by any foreign government.[32] The Department of State has consistently denied that there is any "right" of asylum either in general international law or in any regional rule of law. That position was stated concisely at the Tenth Inter-American Conference (Caracas, 1954) as follows:

... the United States does not recognize or subscribe to the doctrine of asylum as part of international law and does not, in practice, grant asylum except in a very limited sense, ...[33]

This legal position of the United States toward asylum has also been impressed upon U.S. Foreign Service Officers and other diplomatic

---

[31] *Ibid.,* pp. 22-23.

[32] See de Vries and Rodriguez-Novás, *op. cit.,* p. 49.

[33] Tenth Inter-American Conference (Caracas, March, 1954), *Report of the Delegation of the United States of America with Related Documents,* Department of State Publication 5692.

representatives in the formal instructions to American diplomatic officers regularly issued by the State Department. In the 1920's, for example, the relevant article on asylum (included in some instructions issued in 1927) stated that the privilege of immunity from local jurisdiction did not embrace the right of asylum. The following article on "unsanctioned asylum," however, did admit to the occasional practice of granting asylum despite the legal injunction against it:

In some countries, where frequent revolutions occur and consequent instability of government exists, the practice of extraterritorial asylum has been so often resorted to that it has become established to an extent not elsewhere admitted, is virtually recognized by the local government, and is regarded in anticipation as the permissible recourse of unsuccessful insurgents. This Government, which does not look with favor upon such usage, wishes to impress upon its representatives that no encouragement to expect asylum should ever be given. In order that there may be no confusion in their minds it desires to make clear its position as to the nature and extent of the so-called right of asylum and the circumstances in which it may properly be invoked. *The granting of asylum is permissible only to afford temporary shelter to a person under certain conditions of actual danger, and should not be given in the absence of the emergency which would justify such action.* The emergency may arise through imminent danger of mob violence, imminent danger of obviously illegal acts by the duly constituted authorities, or imminent danger of violence at the hands of other agencies, such as revolutionists or persons engaged in an attempt to overthrow the established government. In any case asylum should not be granted if the danger to the person concerned is incurred as a result of criminal activities.[34]

In practice, then, the United States did allow its diplomats in Latin America to grant asylum and even insisted that such asylum, when granted, be respected. As seen above, the justification for this practice of U.S. representatives in the field in contradistinction to the legal position of the U.S. government was "local toleration"; such a policy meant that the United States would *in fact* claim as a right what it did not *in theory* claim as a right.[35] Since the first third of the 20th Century, however, the argument of local toleration has been abandoned as justification for the practice of asylum and humanitarian considerations have been emphasized instead. More recent Foreign Service regulations simply state that asylum may be granted to "uninvited fugitives" whose lives are in imminent danger from mob violence, but only while active

[34] Instructions to Diplomatic Officers of the United States (March, 1927). Quoted in Pfankuchen, Llewellyn, *A Documentary Textbook in International Law,* p. 416. (Italics added.) Rinehart & Co., Inc., New York, 1940.

[35] Ronning, C. Neale, *Law and Politics in Inter-American Diplomacy,* pp. 91-92. John Wiley & Sons, Inc., New York, 1963.

danger continues.[36] In the Cardinal Mindzenti case, the most notable post-war exception to the general U.S. policy of no asylum, the asylum was granted on the basis of humanitarian considerations.

United States policies with regard to the various inter-American conventions on asylum (mentioned above) have been consistent with its legal position. Thus, although the United States signed the 1928 Havana Convention, it stated in a reservation that it did not recognize or subscribe to the doctrine of asylum as a part of international law; furthermore, it did not sign either the Convention of 1933 or that of 1954. The United States, then, unlike its Latin American neighbors, is not bound to the practice of diplomatic asylum and even less to the concept as an element of international law. It therefore may be far more feasible for the United States than for Latin America to take the lead in any regional negotiations or actions designed to limit the right and practice of asylum or the concept of the political offense as a means to discourage the practice of diplonapping. As will be seen in Chapter VIII, the United States was a leading supporter of the 1971 O.A.S. Convention and, in fact, even urged a stronger document.

In concluding this examination, some note should be taken of current developments and trends in the area of international control over criminal acts of private persons which may be considered to be international crimes. In 1920 the Advisory Committee of Jurists which drafted the Statute of the Permanent Court of International Justice recommended the establishment of a High Court of International Justice with jurisdiction to try crimes which constituted breaches of international public order or the universal law of nations. Although the committee also recommended that the Court be given power to define the nature of the crime, fix the penalty, and decide on means of implementing the sentence, the recommendation was rejected by the League as "premature." [37]

A second attempt to institutionalize the concept of international crimes was the 1937 Convention for the Prevention and Punishment of Terrorism and the Convention for the Creation of an International Criminal Court designed to implement the former and to try individuals accused of such terrorism. The Convention on the Court dealt with the criminal responsibility of private persons engaged in terrorism and,

---

[36] Quoted in *ibid.*, p. 93.

[37] García-Mora, Manuel R., *International Responsibility for Hostile Acts of Private Persons Against Foreign States*, p. 179. Martinus Nijhoff, The Hague, 1962.

in fact, established the act of terrorism as an international crime. Signatory states thus agreed both on the establishment of an international criminal court and on the feasibility of making international judgments on matters which were formerly within the jurisdiction of national courts.[38] Although neither convention came into force, they established useful precedents for the possibility of dealing with the diplomatic kidnappings as international crimes susceptible to international adjudication.

A third development in international criminal jurisdiction took place in 1951 when a committee of the U.N. General Assembly adopted the Draft Statute for an International Criminal Court, subsequently considered by the General Assembly as a whole in 1952. According to one analyst, "The proposed Statute represents the most sustained appeal thus far made for an international criminal court with jurisdiction over individuals." [39] Without quoting the Statute in any great detail here, it does provide for an international criminal court which would have competence to try persons accused of crimes "under international law" and, according to interpretation thereof, offenses which they may commit affecting the peace and security of mankind. Among such offenses the encouragement of terrorist activities is included. However, the jurisdiction of the court is severely limited and largely dependent upon the will of the states themselves. Because of these limitations, even its strong proponents conclude that the development of international criminal jurisdiction is hampered by political exigencies and that:

... if an international criminal court is to fulfill its mission of protecting the world community against offenses of individuals directed at its peace and security, a more extensive and independent jurisdiction must be given.[40]

In realistic terms, the granting by states of such international jurisdiction does not appear imminent, to say the least.

From this brief analysis of the status of asylum, extradition, and the political offense, there are both legal conclusions and policy recommendations which may be drawn. Extra-territorial asylum, though not recognized in general international law, is both condoned and followed in Latin America as a matter of regional practice and as provided for among some states by treaty. The "right" of such asylum has been consistently denied by the United States as a matter of law, but has

[38] *Ibid.*, pp. 179-180.
[39] *Ibid.*, p. 181.
[40] *Ibid.*, p. 194.

occasionally been granted by the United States in practice—particularly in Latin America. On the other hand, international law clearly recognizes the right of territorial asylum with usual provisions for the extradition of common criminals. That extradition, however, is generally not granted in the cases of those accused of political offenses. Although extremely vague, the concept of what constitutes a political crime has been both defined and limited to some extent by extradition cases and by practice; such definitions are more negative than positive in that they tend to state what are *not* political offenses by excluding certain acts from that category. Terrorism has generally been so excluded; it has also been designated in various draft conventions as an "international" crime. Moreover, the kidnappings or murders of foreign diplomats are considered to be common crimes under the O.A.S. Convention of 1971 and diplomatic kidnappers are thus specifically liable to extradition.

Although the consideration of various policy recommendations will form a large portion of Chapter VIII, certain preliminary statements can be registered in skeletal form here: 1) Outside of the need to modify the Caracas Asylum Treaty of 1954, there appear to be no insurmountable legal obstacles to curtailing the grant of asylum to prisoners freed in trade for kidnapped diplomats, particularly if there are some doubts as to the political nature of their offenses. Latin American *practice,* however, would have to be severely amended in this respect. 2) The United States is in a peculiar but perhaps advantageous position regarding its own denial of the legal right of extra-territorial asylum which might enable it to act as a political catalyst in this matter. 3) Though extradition proceedings are usually not instituted against those accused of political offenses, they can be exercised against common criminals, terrorists included as such (the diplonappers, as we have seen, clearly fall in this category). This distinction may or may not be relevant for the "political" prisoners actually traded for the diplomats, but it may be applied in the event the kidnappers themselves seek asylum. Extradition for kidnappers has thus been provided for in the O.A.S. Treaty of 1971 and could be included in other wider international agreements. 4) Recent developments in *international* criminal law, although of little immediate relevance, may reflect some growing tendency on the part of the international community to define, prevent, and/or prosecute certain acts of private individuals as international crimes liable to international adjudication. Such a trend could avert some of the more obvious pitfalls of purely national actions in matters of international concern.

CHAPTER V

KIDNAPPING ATTEMPTS AND RANSOM TRADES

The old concept of diplomats as "striped-pants cookie-pushers" received its first blow in the aftermath of World War II when the world diplomatic corps—and particularly that of the United States—was greatly expanded. This growth was due not only to the need to reassume the traditional diplomatic contacts interrupted by the war years, but also to deal with the vast host of countries catapulted into the international arena in the wake of war, revolution, and receding colonialism. The sudden expansion of the "international community" brought into focus new problems of economic and political development which demanded new techniques and new people. Along with the striped-pants ambassadors and their retinues came the "shirt-sleeve diplomats" to tackle the gritty and seemingly insoluble dilemmas of the third world—its poverty, its misery, and its growing aspirations. This new breed of diplomats was soon absorbed within the diplomatic missions, and amended rules and regulations concerning their privileges and immunities, if any, gradually emerged.

The second challenge to the mistaken image of diplomacy as a sort of sissified child's-play [1] has been the increasing number of attacks and assaults on foreign representatives overseas, many of them resulting in serious injuries and, in some cases, even death. Although diplomacy in fact, if not in fiction, has never been devoid of such hazards, it has faced increased difficulties in its attempts to operate in the unsettled atmosphere of the newly emerging states of Africa and Asia and in the political turmoil of Latin America. In these areas where the politics of debate and reason are frequently sublimated in the politics of terrorism

---

[1] In 1950, for example, Senator Joseph Mc Carthy referred to "dilettante diplomats" who do their fighting "with kid gloves in perfumed drawing rooms." *New York Times,* June 18, 1950.

and assassination not only the national politician but also the foreign diplomat must face the dangers of those uncertainties. It is a climate hardly conducive to peace of mind—and the current vogue of diplonappings has made it less so.

According to a survey made in 1967,[2] "At least thirteen diplomatic, quasi-diplomatic, and consular personnel have been killed since 1947, including five Americans, five nationals assigned to United States establishments, one British subject, one Spaniard, and one Turk."[3] Of these, five were killed in the Middle East, five in Vietnam, one in Ethiopia, one in Mexico, and one in the Soviet Union. Six deaths occurred as a result of terrorist bombings and at least another six resulted from shootings of one sort or another. The survey points out that during the same period and in addition to the cases just mentioned, numerous other diplomatic agents and staff members were subjected to attack, assault, insults, and other indignities and injuries not resulting in death. These included both diplomatic agents whose diplomatic inviolability was infringed upon by government representatives and a far larger number of diplomatic agents who were the victims of actions taken by unofficial personnel in the host states. The violations usually occurred as the result of mob assaults, internal strife, or such individual actions as sniping, attempted assassination, etc.

As Chapters II and III have indicated, international law clearly provides that diplomatic personnel possess diplomatic inviolability and that, as a result of such inviolability, the host government is under a special obligation to protect them. Receiving states, in fact, may be held strictly accountable for the murder or killing of diplomats within their territories.[4] If such murders occur despite their protective efforts the host governments may be called upon to afford satisfactory redress in the form of official apologies, prosecution and punishment of the offenders, and/or indemnities and reparations. In the cases mentioned above these various legal forms of redress were resorted to in practice.

Thus, in a Cypriot case involving the death of an American Vice-Consul by terrorist bombs, the Greek delegation to the U.N. referred to the killing with "shock and sorrow" and E.O.K.A., the Greek Cypriot

[2] The data in the following four paragraphs are drawn from Wilson, Clifton E., *Diplomatic Privileges And Immunities,* pp. 51-62. University of Arizona Press, Tucson, Arizona, 1967.

[3] *Ibid.,* pp. 52-53.

[4] Plischke, Elmer, *Conduct of American Diplomacy* (2nd Ed.), p. 336. D. Van Nostrand Co., Princeton, N.J., 1961.

underground, assumed full blame for the action and expressed "deep regret" for the terrible misfortune. Three Cypriots were subsequently arrested. Similarly, in a terrorist bombing in Damascus, the Syrian Government expressed both sympathy and abhorrence over the death of an employee in the U.S.I.S. building. Moreover, the Syrian Army Chief of Staff stated that he would do his utmost to arrest and punish those responsible. In terms of actual punishment, when a Spanish diplomat was gunned down on a Mexican street in 1950, the Cuban responsible for the shooting was ultimately sentenced to sixteen years in prison. Of these cases, the only public report of monetary compensation made was that paid by Iraq to Britain for the murder of the British Military Attaché of the British Embassy in Baghdad.

These selected cases would seem to illustrate that when diplomatic immunity is violated by the murder of foreign diplomats, host governments have generally responded positively and in accordance with the rules of international law to attempt to provide adequate redress to the injured state. Of equal interest are the "threats" of assassination which have been issued to diplomats by those opposing them personally or, more frequently, by those opposed to the policies of the diplomat's home government. Such threats have been most common in Latin America and are consistent with the prevalence of diplomatic kidnappings in those countries. In most of these cases of assassination threats, the host governments acted quickly to carry out their obligations of protection. Thus, in 1948, the Cuban Government stated that it had taken "precautionary measures" to prevent reported death plots against the U.S. and Mexican Ambassadors; in 1951 the Spanish Government warned the U.S. Ambassador about an assassination plot and assigned four plainclothesmen to keep a constant watch on him; and, in 1960, the U.S. Government stated that Castro agents had been assigned to assassinate the United States Ambassador to Mexico and, as a result, special details of Mexican police were assigned to protect him for over a year. Moreover, as a result of such threats, diplomats were also instructed to take precautionary measures on their own. For example, in 1950 the U.S. State Department reported that it had ordered diplomats in certain parts of Southeast Asia to carry guns for their own protection.[5] Such unilateral directives may come increasingly into vogue as necessary precautions in the unsettled political climate of Latin America. Some, indeed, already have.

---

[5] Reported in *New York Times,* June 18, 1950.

Turning to the diplonapping cases themselves, these may be categorized either according to their basic purpose or according to their ultimate outcome. In terms of purpose, some of the diplomatic kidnappings were undertaken for traditional ransom in the sense of a monetary sum to be paid for the release of the kidnapped diplomats. Others—and, in fact, the majority—were more complicated in that they sought not a monetary payment, but the exchange of a certain number of designated "political prisoners" for the diplomat's release. In either case the diplomat himself became a sort of political pawn in the hands of the diplonappers who were using him for their own monetary or political purposes. The diplonappers were primarily attempting to provoke certain reactions by their own government rather than by that of the diplomat in question. His capture was usually not related either to his own activities or to the policies of his own government; it was simply a function of his position as a diplomat whose protection was supposedly guaranteed by his host government. These host governments themselves, therefore, as well as their funds and/or policies have been and are the targets of the diplonappings.

Analyzing the diplonapping cases according to their outcome produces four possible categories: 1) those in which a kidnapping attempt was made, but failed (information on these is scant and little can be ascertained as to motives involved); 2) diplonappings which did "succeed" in the sense that a diplomat or other governmental agent was kidnapped and ransom was paid or political prisoners were traded for his release; 3) diplonappings in which the kidnapping occurred but demands were not met and the diplomat was nonetheless released unharmed; and 4) diplonappings in which the kidnapping took place but subsequent demands were not met and the diplomatic agent was then murdered.[6] Most of the cases in Categories One through Three will be examined here in Chapter V; because of the need for greater detail, Chapter VI will examine most of the Category Four cases as a separate section, and Chapter VII will be devoted to the Canadian kidnappings which are *sui generis*. Although some mention will be made of a few of the publicized diplonapping attempts which failed, greater attention

---

[6] A fifth possible category might include those kidnappings in which no demands were made. Although a 1963 kidnapping of the deputy head of the U.S. Military Mission in Venezuela apparently fell into that category, none of the 1968-1972 series of diplomatic kidnappings were made without demands and therefore this analysis has been limited to the four categories listed.

will be devoted to those which "succeeded" and to the different governmental policies pursued towards them.

An abortive kidnapping attempt of two Soviet diplomats took place in Argentina on March 29, 1970,[7] when four men, members of a right-wing extremist group, MANO (Argentine National Organized Movement), ambushed the two Embassy officials in a commercial garage as they were returning from a family drive. One of the diplomats fell from the car as it drove off and the other, Yuri Pivovarov, was rescued when the car crashed after a police chase. Three of the assailants were injured and captured; the fourth escaped. MANO, which claimed responsibility for the kidnapping, had earlier threatened to kill the Soviet Ambassador to Argentina in reprisal for the leftist kidnapping of a Paraguayan Consul on March 24th.[8] The Soviet Union issued a formal protest note to the Argentine Government which responded with an apology and a statement which blamed the action on gangsters and armed delinquents. Although one of the wounded kidnappers was identified as a deputy federal police inspector, with right-wing beliefs, President Onganiá of Argentina maintained that the Argentine Government had not been involved and he ordered an investigation of the entire incident.

A second fairly recent case in which an apparent kidnapping attempt was foiled was that involving the U.S. Consul in Porto Alegre, Brazil, Curtis C. Cutter.[9] When several armed men attacked and jumped his car in early April, 1970, Cutter swerved abruptly to throw them off his vehicle and, driving over one of them, escaped with only a shoulder wound. Since this attempt followed in the wake of the highly publicized von Spreti murder in Guatemala,[10] Cutter's quick reaction was not only admirable, but understandable. This attempted abduction nonetheless increased the concern and anxiety of the United States Government over the security of its diplomatic and consular personnel overseas.

An earlier kidnapping attempt took place in August, 1968, when the United States Ambassador to Guatemala, John Gordan Mein, was assassinated by unidentified assailants who ambushed his limousine.[11] A statement signed by the major Communist guerilla organization in

[7] Reported in *Facts on File* (April 2-8, 1970) and in the *New York Times,* March 30, 1970.

[8] See below, pp. 85-86.

[9] *New York Times,* April 6, 1970.

[10] See Chapter VI.

[11] The following account is based on reports in the *New York Times,* August 29, 30 and September 6, 1968.

Guatemala, the F.A.R., admitted responsibility for the assassination and confirmed speculation that it had intended to kidnap the Ambassador as a pawn in trade for an imprisoned guerilla leader; Mein was killed when he resisted capture. The U.S. State Department requested "a full investigation of all the circumstances" surrounding the event from the Guatemalan Government which immediately proclaimed a state of martial law. Later the Government stated that the assassins of Mein had been identified, and it offered a $10,000 reward for information leading to their arrest. As will be seen below, Guatemala has been the scene not only for unsuccessful abduction attempts, but for the tragic kidnapping and killing of the West German Ambassador, Count Karl von Spreti.

The second category of diplonapping cases encompasses those in which diplomats were kidnapped and either ransom was paid or political prisoners were exchanged for their release. Four of these cases—three highly publicized—took place in Brazil where in each instance the Brazilian Government ultimately acceded to the demands of the diplo-nappers. This is of special interest in light of the Brazilian position in favor of a hardline policy of "no asylum" for any released political prisoners which they argued in the O.A.S. discussions of June, 1970. What were the national circumstances which made this terrorist technique of diplo-napping blackmail so effective in Brazil? Since 1964 Brazil had been under the control of a military Junta which had overthrown President João Goulart in that year. During that time the pendulum had wavered between military repression on the one hand and guerilla terrorism on the other. The Brazilian Constitution had been set aside and the legislature disbanded; political parties had been abolished and political and civil rights suspended; the mass media were consistently censored and nongovernmental organizations and associations frequently repressed.[12] In addition, allegations of torture and arbitrary incarceration of sus-pected terrorists ran rampant and, in fact, early in December, 1970, the Brazilian Minister of Education publicly admitted the use of torture by Brazilian security forces.[13]

In reaction to such repression—and as catalytic measures designed to foster even harsher governmental retaliation—the guerillas escalated their terror from the robbing of banks and bombing of barracks to the "execution" of government officials and the kidnapping of foreign

[12] *New York Times,* December 13, 1970, and *Time Magazine,* December 21, 1970. See also Chapter I: Urban Terrorism in Revolutionary Strategy.
[13] *New York Times,* December 13, 1970.

emisarries. In contrast to prophesies of early failure, the urban guerillas in Brazil have spread their influence and made their impact upon the body politic through terror, if not through votes. The emphasis on revolution as a way of life—and death—was highlighted in the statement of principles which supposedly reflected the attitudes of the seventy prisoners who were freed in exchange for Swiss Ambassador Bucher in 1970: "We who were born revolutionaries will die as revolutionaries." [14]

In late 1968 the level of conflict had been heightened when right-wing military elements gained ascendancy in the Brazilian Government and issued by decree the Fifth Institutional Act which greatly increased arbitrary rule. After that time, the abrogation of habeas corpus, increased police roundups, arrests without warrants, and imprisonments without trial became widespread.[15] Within this context revolutionary activities, rather than abating, flowered into full bloom. By 1971 approximately fifteen different revolutionary groups were operating in Brazil. As has been pointed out in Chapter I, the most significant of these was the National Liberation Action or Alliance (A.L.N.), founded by Carlos Marighella in 1967-68. With its emphasis upon urban guerilla terrorism directed against the Government, the A.L.N. also sought to use guerilla warfare to develop political awareness among the masses. The second most important revolutionary group, the Peoples' Revolutionary Vanguard or V.R.P., differed from the A.L.N. in regarding itself as a revolutionary vanguard whose military victory would have to precede the establishment of an elected government. Both groups sought to achieve the revolutionary overthrow of the military regime in power.

This brief background sketch may help to clarify the political and social climate within which the Brazilian diplonappings of 1969-1971 took place. The so-called "Elbrick case" [16] occurred in 1969 when, on September 3, the United States Ambassador to Brazil was kidnapped on the streets of Rio de Janeiro by four armed men. The diplonappers issued a three-page manifesto which contained two demands and a threat to kill the Ambassador if their demands were not met. The two urban guerilla bands which signed the manifesto demanded: 1) that fifteen

---

[14] Quoted in *The Milwaukee Journal,* January 16, 1971.

[15] The following analysis is based largely upon an article in the *New York Times,* December 13, 1970.

[16] The following paragraph is based on the report in the *New York Times,* September 5, 1969.

unnamed political prisoners be released and flown to political exile in Chile, Mexico, or Algeria and 2) that the full text of the anti-Government manifesto be published throughout the mass media. The kidnapping was regarded as part of the terrorist campaign then being carried on by the two revolutionary groups. September 5th, the Brazilian National Security Council [17] authorized the newspapers to print the text of the manifesto but at the same time declared the kidnapping to be "an act of pure and simple terrorism." In addition, although not publicized before their release, the fifteen Brazilian political prisoners were freed by the Government and flown to Mexico City where they were granted full political asylum.[18] According to an AP dispatch, thirteen of the fifteen subsequently decided to go to Cuba.[19]

The Elbrick diplonapping thus occurred in the midst of an extremely volatile political situation and can best be understood in the context of widespread terrorist activities throughout the country. Though the terrorism and the kidnapping itself were aimed primarily at the Brazilian military government, the kidnappers stated in another manifesto issued after the release of Elbrick that although they had "nothing personal" against Mr. Elbrick, as Ambassador of the United States he did represent the interests of the "big North American capitalists" which collided head-on with those of the people. Elbrick himself stated, "These guys had no interest in hurting me but I didn't know it." [20] This element of uncertainty, of course, is what the kidnappers rely on to persuade the host government to accede to their demands. Unfortunately, as evidenced both in the von Spreti case in Guatemala and in the Mitrione case in Uruguay, their threats to kill the abducted hostage have not always been empty ones.

Following the release of Ambassador Elbrick,[21] the Brazilian Government established the death penalty for cases of revolutionary or subversive warfare, increased the police powers of the armed forces, and instructed the military police to investigate the entire kidnapping. It was sub-

---

[17] Headed by three military ministers and acting on behalf of the then stricken President Arthur da Costa e Silva.

[18] *New York Times,* September 8, 1969.

[19] AP dispatch of September 29. Reported in the *New York Times,* September 30, 1969.

[20] Quoted in the *New York Times,* September 8, 1969.

[21] The following paragraph is based largely on accounts in the *New York Times,* October 3, November 5, and December 20, 1969, and January 18 and February 4, 1970.

sequently alleged that these police forces both threatened and used torture on those suspected of connection with the responsible guerilla groups. In November, 1969, it was reported that the police shot and killed Carlos Marighella, the terrorist said to have planned the Elbrick kidnapping and leader of the National Liberation Action. Marighella was also the author of the urban guerilla "Minimanual" which has been widely distributed and read among terrorist groups in Latin America. The following month a student, Claudio Torres de Silva, was sentenced to ten years of imprisonment for his part in the kidnapping; three more persons were being held at that time on charges of complicity in the plot. Finally, in February, 1970, the Brazilian army announced that eighteen persons had been involved in planning and carrying out the Elbrick diplonapping; of these, four had been arrested in Brazil and faced trial in the military courts. Others were said to have fled and to be in hiding in Cuba.

In a speech before the World Affairs Council of Philadelphia on June 8, 1971,[22] Ambassador Elbrick reflected on his kidnapping and provided some additional insights into the motivations of his kidnappers. About an hour after his capture, he had been closely interrogated about the activities, members, and contacts of the CIA in Brazil by two men brought in from the outside whom he regarded as " . . . obviously Communists—unlike the kidnappers themselves who did not claim to be Communists." Asserting that the United States was the "enemy number one" of the Brazilian people, they regarded the Brazilian Government as a "lackey" of the United States and Elbrick as a pawn to be used in exchange for demands on the Brazilian Government. In terms of the kidnappers' intentions, Ambassador Elbrick stated that he never had any doubt that he would be shot if anything went wrong.

When questioned regarding what could be done to prevent future kidnappings, Elbrick commended the resolution adopted by the O.A.S. Council in February, 1971, which declared the kidnappings of government officials to be common crimes and hence their perpetrators extraditable. In addition, he declared that although it would have resulted in his own "disappearance from the scene," it would be "unwise" for a government to negotiate with terrorists and to give in to any of their demands. He admitted, however, that several diplomats might have to "disappear" before the kidnappers got the message that governments

---

[22] "Diplomats in Danger." Tape of speech by Ambassador C. Burke Elbrick to World Affairs Council of Philadelphia on June 8, 1971.

were not willing to give any ransom or prisoners in such an exchange. Ambassador Elbrick was less than optimistic about the prospects of protecting all diplomats everywhere. He pointed out some of the short-comings of diplomats being surrounded constantly by guards and also emphasized the dangers involved in arming them. These and other proposals for protection are discussed in Chapter VIII.

A second notable Brazilian case of diplonapping took place in June, 1970, and involved the abduction of the Ambassador of the German Federal Republic to Brazil, Ehrenfried von Holleben.[23] The kidnapping of von Holleben received considerable publicity because it followed by only two and one-half months the kidnapping and murder of another West German Ambassador, Count von Spreti, the envoy to Guatemala. Ambassador von Holleben was kidnapped en route from the German Embassy to his home by eight "urban guerillas," once again members of the two revolutionary groups who indicated that they would ask for the release of political prisoners in exchange; they did not originally specify any by name or indicate how many they would request. The Government immediately stated that it would do all it could to save von Holleben's life and obtain his safe release; moreover, the Brazilian President, Emilio Garrastazu Medici, went to Rio de Janeiro to direct personally the search for the Ambassador. It was generally anticipated, therefore, that the Brazilian Government would meet the kidnappers' demand for the release of the political prisoners.

According to a Rio de Janeiro newspaper, Brazilian security officials had discovered a plot to capture von Holleben some 45 days prior to his actual abduction, but after making some fifty arrests they thought they had broken the effort.[24] Nonetheless, special precautions had clearly been taken in that a station wagon carrying security men was following the Ambassador's car when he was abducted and another security agent, stationed in the front seat of von Holleben's car, was fatally wounded in the kidnapping. Since the kidnappers' statement maintained that they would not "discriminate" in the future as to the states whose diplomats they might abduct, it is not surprising that the *New York Times* reported that there was "an aura of tenseness" among other ambassadors in Brazil.

The position of the German Federal Republic was made quite clear. In Bonn, West German Foreign Minister Walter Scheel stated that the

---

[23] The following account is based on reports in the *New York Times,* June 12, 13, and 14, 1970.

[24] Reported in the *New York Times,* June 13, 1970.

German Government would take "all possible steps" to secure von Holleben's safe return. It had instructed its aides to use not only conventional but also unconventional channels to make contact with the diplonappers. When von Holleben was ultimately freed, the West German Embassy in Brazil stated that it had believed that the Brazilian Government should take the same position it had taken in previous kidnappings —obviously alluding to the Elbrick case. Von Holleben himself, prior to his abduction, had commented on the von Spreti incident in Guatemala and had criticized the policy of the Guatemalan Government in having refused to grant the kidnappers' request on "constitutional grounds"; he argued instead that the international law which protected diplomats should prevail over domestic legal considerations.

On June 14, 1970, the Brazilian Government publicly accepted all of the demands of the diplonappers, including the release of forty political prisoners who were to be granted asylum in Mexico, Chile, or Algeria and the mass media publication of their revolutionary manifesto by press and radio. The manifesto contained a detailed statement of the guerilla aims, a review of the Brazilian social, economic, and political situation, and accusations of government repression. The Government published the manifesto, rounded up the forty prisoners, and stated that they would be flown directly from Brazil to Algeria and released there. The guerillas then indicated that they would free the Ambassador after news releases and radio photographs transmitted by international news agencies had confirmed that the prisoners had actually arrived in Algeria. The forty prisoners landed in Algiers on June 15; the Algerian Government stated that they would be granted asylum there for "humanitarian reasons." At a news conference following their release the prisoners maintained that they had been tortured while in jail and had been made to believe that they were to be executed.

Ambassador von Holleben was freed the following evening, June 16; the release was apparently deplayed about 24 hours because the diplonappers believed police vigilance in Rio de Janeiro was too strict. As a result, street patrols were subsequently reduced. Following his release, the Ambassador said:

I feel happy and grateful to the Brazilian government for the steps they took for my return safe and sound to my family. I offer salutation to the people and government of Brazil.

In addition, the West German Embassy issued a communique which stated:

In this hour of happpiness, the family of the ambassador as well as all the Embassy's members, feel the great duty of transmitting to the Brazilian government, especially to his excellency the president (Emilio Garrastazu Medici) of the republic, the deep gratitude for the measures which were taken to get the release of our ambasador."[25]

The Government of the German Federal Republic in Bonn also made it clear that it was satisfied with the actions taken by the Brazilian Government in the entire matter. This German position stood out in stark contrast to their attitude toward the Guatemalan Government in the von Spreti affair.

Despite increased Government security efforts, the von Holleben kidnapping did not mark the end of diplonapping in Brazil. In early November, 1970, authorities specifically clamped down on the National Liberation Alliance with the arrests of over 5,000 people suspected of subversive activities. The Government went so far as to announce that this measure had frustrated a plan by the A.L.N. to attempt a number of abductions in commemoration of the death of its founder, Carlos Marighella, who had been killed in a police ambush the year before. Details of the kidnapping plans were allegedly found in the apartment of Marighella's successor, then leader of the A.L.N., who died in November.[26] With his death, Brazilian military leaders as well as several foreign observers believed that the National Liberation Alliance had been defeated and that any future political kidnappings had thus been prevented. Their predictions were proven wrong just one month later when the third major diplonapping in Brazil took place.

In early December, 1970, the Swiss Ambassador to Brazil, Giovanni Enrico Bucher, was kidnapped by members of the Peoples' Revolutionary Vanguard (V.R.P.) which along with the A.L.N. had been involved in at least three other Brazilian kidnappings, including the Elbrick and von Holleben abduction.[27] The ambush was carried out by six or seven commandos armed with submachine guns; although Ambassador Bucher was not injured, his bodyguard, a Brazilian federal agent, was mortally wounded by gunshots. A roadblock was immediately set up around Rio de Janeiro and a car identified as one of the four used in the kidnapping was apprehended; Bucher himself, however, was not found. The Swiss

---

[25] UPI dispatch. Quoted in *The Milwaukee Journal,* June 17, 1970.

[26] Reported in the *New York Times,* December 8 and 13, 1970.

[27] The following account is based on reports in the *New York Times,* December 8-15. *The Washington Post, The Milwaukee Journal,* and *The Globe and Mail* (Toronto) have also been consulted for corroboration.

Government in Bern dispatched a diplomatic note to the Brazilian Government demanding "immediate steps" to secure the release of Ambassador Bucher and continuous close contact was subsequently maintained by the Swiss with the Brazilian authorities. Speculation as to why Bucher had been selected for the abduction centered on the fact that Switzerland had recently expelled two Brazilian terrorists who had been included among the forty prisoners freed by Brazil in exchange for the release of Ambassador von Holleben. Probably of equal importance was the fact that Bucher, as Swiss Ambassador, possessed an important exchange value for Brazil. Next to the United States and Germany, Switzerland and Japan are the third most important investors in Brazil.

As in the Elbrick and von Holleben cases, the urban guerillas quickly sought to negotiate a bargain with the Brazilian Government whereby a specified number of "political prisoners" would be released in exchange for the captured diplomat. The kidnappers of Ambassador Bucher demanded that seventy such prisoners accused of terrorism and subversion be released and be allowed to fly to exile in Chile, Algeria, or Mexico, in that order of preference. This was the highest ransom yet asked for a single diplomat. In addition, three other conditions included: broadcast of an anti-Government manifesto on all radio and TV stations for two consecutive days, publication in the press of pictures of all released prisoners, and immediate publication of all rebel communiques by the press. Ignoring the demands for publicity, Brazilian government officials indicated that they would accept terms involving the release of prisoners—even if they numbered as many as seventy. After the President, Emilio Garrastazu Medici, conferred with the Ministers of Justice and Foreign Affairs and the heads of the three armed forces, a communique was issued which stated that the Government would negotiate as soon as it received a hand-written, dated, and signed note from Ambassador Bucher with a list of the prisoners to be freed. The Brazilian Government also indicated that if it received no "authentic communication" from Bucher it would take new measures to secure his quick release.

After a flurry of unconfirmed reports that various prisoner lists had been submitted and rejected and during which time over 2,500 government soldiers intensively but unsuccessfully searched jungle-covered sections of Rio, Brazilian authorities agreed to release fifty-one of the seventy prisoners specified in a message which had been co-signed by Bucher and sent to the Government on December 19, 1970; Government spokesmen said it could not release the nineteen others since some were quilty of such nonpolitical crimes as murder and kidnapping.[28] (Moreover, the Government also indicated that it was gathering medical information on the prisoners to counter expected charges of government torture if and when they were released.) [29] Following the Government's offer, there was no immediate response from the diplonappers. but negotiations continued over which prisoners would or would not be released. Authorities returned three different lists of prisoners before agreement was reached. However, a little less than a month later a total of seventy prisoners was ultimately freed and flown to exile in Chile where they were granted political asylum.[30] Photographs of their arrival were published in Rio newspapers on January 14, 1971. Brazilian President Garrastazu Medici had signed a decree the previous day authorizing the banishment of sixty-eight prisoners of Brazilian citizenship and the deportation of two foreign prisoners. It was later reported that the guerilla demands for publication of their political manifesto had been refused and that the Government had finally agreed to release only "political prisoners" as ransom.[31] The head of Chile's police force warned the political exiles upon their arrival:

During your stay in Chile, you will not make political statements nor any other statements which could damage the good relations between Chile and other countries.[32]

Two days after the Brazilian prisoners arrived in Chile, Ambassador Bucher was released unharmed in dowtown Rio.[33] In the interim, Brazilian police had instituted an extremely heavy guard patrol throughout the city in the hope of arresting the kidnappers prior to Bucher's release; these attempts were manifestly unsuccessful and after he was freed the Ambassador indicated that he had been blindfolded when captured and had no idea of where he had been held captive. He thanked the Brazilian Government for having helped him—obviously

[28] Reported in the *New York Times,* December 22, 1970, and *The Milwaukee Journal,* December 22, 1970.

[29] Several of the prisoners who were ultimately released in exchange for Bucher's freedom voiced accusations of both psychological and physical torture having been applied while they were in jail. *The Milwaukee Journal,* January 16, 1971.

[30] The *New York Times,* January 15, 1971.

[31] *The Milwaukee Journal,* January 16, 1971.

[32] Quoted in *ibid.,* January 14, 1971.

[33] Reported in the *New York Times,* January 17, 1971, and *The Milwaukee Journal,* January 16, 1971.

by having agreed to trade the prisoners for his release. If these seventy prisoners are added to those traded earlier for Elbrick, Okuchi (see below), and von Holleben, there was a grand total of 130 Brazilian prisoners who were released by the Brazilian Government in exchange for four kidnapped diplomats in 1970 and early 1971.

Three other examples of diplonappings which resulted in the exchange of political prisoners for kidnapped diplomats also took place in 1970. In March, Lt. Col. Donald J. Crowley,[34] an Air Attaché at the U.S. Embassy in Santo Domingo, the Dominican Republic, was abducted by a group of guerillas who threatened to kill him if twenty political prisoners were not released by the Government according to an announced deadline. Although the Chief of Police initiated an active search for Crowley, the Government of the Dominican Republic finally acceded to the threat, took twenty prisoners to the Mexican Embassy under armed guard, and authorized an airliner to fly them to Mexico where they went into political exile. Lt. Col. Crowley was subsequently released unharmed.

In Guatemala the same month, Sean M. Holly,[35] a political secretary in the U.S. Embassy, was kidnapped by five armed men of the guerilla Rebel Armed Forces group which threatened to "execute" Holly if the government would not release four political prisoners. Although one was not a prisoner, he and two others received temporary asylum in the Costa Rican Embassy and all four asylum in Mexico. Holly was released after the political prisoners were freed. Also in March, the Japanese Consul-General in São Paulo, Brazil, was kidnapped by Brazilian terrorists and released only after the Government freed five political prisoners and allowed them to seek political asylum in Mexico.[36]

A somewhat different case falling within this second category of "successful" diplonappings was that involving an armed attack on the Swiss Consul in Colombia in early October, 1969.[37] The Consul was seriously wounded and his fifteen-year-old son and the first secretary of the Swiss Embassy were kidnapped. This case differed from the

[34] The Crowley account is based on reports in the *New York Times*, March 25 and 27, 1970. An erroneous report that the Guatemalan Chief of Police had taken over the search for Crowley was rectified by Crowley in a letter of June 1, 1971, to the author.

[35] Reported in the *New York Times*, March 7 and April 1, 1970.

[36] Reported in the *New York Times*, April 1, 1970. Consul-General Okuchi's kidnapping was one of the four Brazilian cases mentioned.

[37] Reported in the *New York Times*, October 7, 11, and 23, 1969.

preceding examples in that $300,000 ransom was demanded for their freedom instead of the release of any political prisoners. The Colombian Government imposed a condition of "siege" in the state of Valle de Cauco in an attempt to halt what the *New York Times* referred to as "a wave of kidnappings" in which eight persons had been kidnapped and a total of $600,000 paid in ransom between August and October. The police arrested four men in connection with the kidnappings although they made no specific charges and indicated that they had no immediate clues as to the whereabouts of those kidnapped. Later in the month, however, the diplonappers released the two Swiss citizens and the Colombian Government stated that the kidnappers had received "considerable ransom"; the exact amount was not specified. Evidently, here again, the threats issued were sufficient to induce the host government to respond affirmatively.

Finally, what might be regarded as a "quasi-diplomatic" kidnapping of the Category Two variety took place in Argentina on May 23, 1971, when the British Honorary Consul in Rosario, Mr. Stanley M. F. Sylvester, was kidnapped by three young terrorists.[38] A note signed by the Revolutionary Army of the People stated that Sylvester would be tried before "a people's court of justice" but there were no ransom demands for his release made at that time. The quasi-diplomatic nature of the kidnapping arises from the fact that Mr. Sylvester was not only an honorary consul (Argentine-born), but the manager of Rosario's large Swift de la Plata meat packing plant which had laid off a large proportion of its 15,000 workers in late 1970. Speculation that the kidnapping had less to do with Mr. Sylvester's diplomatic position than with his position as manager of the Swift plant was confirmed a few days later when ransom demands were made for the distribution of $62,500 worth of food and clothing to the poor and for better working conditions.

The Argentine Government replied with a major search by police and army forces throughout Rosario, but the kidnappers were not uncovered. Meanwhile, although no reply was made to the demand for better working conditions, plant sources indicated that food would be distributed to the poor. When this was subsequently done, Mr. Sylvester was released. Despite its early conclusion, however, the kidnapping proved a source of some embarrassment to the Argentine Government not only because of the no ransom policy which had been followed in

---

[38] Account based on reports in the *New York Times,* May 24, 29, 31, 1971, and in *The Christian Science Monitor,* May 26, 1971.

the case of Paraguayan Consul Waldemar Sanchez (see below), but also because of its contention that terrorism in Argentina had lessened in recent months. The highly-publicized $300,000 bank robbery which took place in Córdoba in February, an abortive military revolt in early May, continuing labor unrest, and the spread of the urban guerilla activities of the ERP throughout the country, seemed to indicate that Argentina, like Brazil and Uruguay, remained politically volatile, unstable and highly susceptible to urban terrorism.

The third category of diplonappings includes those cases in which the government concerned did *not* accede to the kidnappers' demands, but the diplomats in question were released unharmed in spite of that fact. Such cases are few indeed, particularly in Latin America. From a fairly extensive examination of recent newspaper and periodical accounts of terrorism, assassinations, and kidnappings in Latin America, for example, Argentina alone emerged as the one Latin American country which had successfully defied the diplonappers.

In March, 1970—at the same general time when the governments of Brazil, the Dominican Republic, and Guatemala were freeing political prisoners in exchange for a Consul-General, an Air Attaché, and a political secretary respectively—the Argentine Government faced the kidnappers of Waldemar Sanchez, a consul of Paraguay, with a flat refusal to trade Sanchez for "two political prisoners." [39] The diplonappers were members of the left-wing Argentine Liberation Command front who claimed that Sanchez was a known agent of the CIA and a representative of the Stroessner dictatorship; they threatened to kill him if the prisoner(s) were not released. Although Argentine President Juan Carlos Onganiá rejected their demands, the kidnappers freed Sanchez for, as they said, "humanitarian reasons" without obtaining the release of the prisoners. Thus, according to the *New York Times*, the Argentine Government was the first successfully to refuse to accede to the Latin American terrorist demands.

In an attempt to elicit additional information regarding the attitudes of the Argentine Government and the basis for its refusal to release the two prisoners, the author contacted the Argentine Embassy in Washington, D.C., and received a non-official translation of two official

---

[39] The following account of the Sánchez kidnapping is based on reports in the *New York Times*, March 25 and 29, 1970. According to the government, as will be seen, only one of the two specified men was actually a prisoner at the time; the second was being sought.

communiqués from the Argentine Government to its Embassy in Washington.[40] Communiqué No. 1 stated that one of the two designated men was in fact a fugitive from justice who was being intensively sought under an order of arrest. The second man was being prosecuted for "nonpolitical" crimes by the Federal Court of San Martin, Province of Buenos Aires. The Government stated that it would be against the principle of justice to set him free since his case was not under the jurisdiction of the Executive Branch of Government.

The second communiqué reasserted the Government's claim that the one supposed "prisoner" was actually a fugitive being sought by the police "in connection with terrorist activities and assaulting . . . a military unit." Stating that it deeply regretted the fact that the life of a citizen and diplomatic officer of Paraguay was being threatened by these events, the Government nonetheless reiterated its "firm decision" to submit to the national penal law the case of the second man: " . . . to try to make him escape the decision or verdict of the courts, will be a detriment to the justice and the order which should govern every organized society." This position, though not identical, was parallel to the Guatemalan Government's position when it refused to free "condemned" prisoners for the release of German Ambassador Karl von Spreti; both Governments justified their refusals on the basis of domestic law and legal procedures. The wider implications of the Argentine policy of "no ransom" will be analyzed in Chapter VIII.

Three other cases of apparent success for policies of no ransom took place in Spain and in Turkey in late 1970 and in early 1971 respectively. In early December, 1970, the Honorary West German Consul in San Sebastian, Eugen Beihl, was kidnapped in Spain by a splinter faction of the Basque guerillas (E.T.A.). The E.T.A. group sought to prevent a predicted verdict of six death sentences in a Burgos court-martial of fifteen Basques accused of a 1968 murder of the provincial head of the Political Police.[41] The highly publicized trial had burgeoned into a symbolic struggle between the Basques—an ethnic minority in North Central Spain—and the central Government in Madrid. Although leaders of the E.T.A. first disavowed involvement in the kidnapping and, in fact,

---

[40] Secretary of Embassy of the Argentine Republic, Letter to Dr. Carol Edler Baumann, October 20, 1970. Attached: Communiqué No. 1 and Communiqué No. 2 (Undated).

[41] The following account is drawn largely from the *New York Times,* December 3-6, 1970.

voiced their belief that it might be counterproductive and actually increase the chances that the death penalty would be invoked, Consul Beihl indicated in his first communication that "the E.T.A." was holding him prisoner and that the German Embassy should do what it asked.[42]

Meanwhile, strikes and demonstrations protesting the court-martial of the fifteen Basque prisoners had broken out *en masse* in Guipúzcoa, the Basque province from which Beihl had been abducted. A three-month state of emergency was then decreed under which the police were given special powers to search without warrant and to hold suspects indefinitely without court hearings; a house to house search for Beihl was conducted in San Sebastian under the decree. The declaration of a state of emergency was the first formal response of the Franco Government both to the Basque disaffection and to the kidnapping and it seemed to indicate the assumption of a hard-line stance. This was taken despite the pleas for clemency from the Vatican, Spanish bishops, and even some top Army officers who opposed the use of Army court-martials for political crimes. It appeared evident that the Franco regime found itself in a political impasse between capitulation to rebel pressures on the one hand and equally strong opposition to the policy of repression upon which it had already embarked. Nonetheless, speculation arose that the Government hoped to avoid measures which might exacerbate the entire situation and provoke the kidnappers to any extreme reprisal.

Just three days before Christmas, 1970, Basque spokesmen stated that an agreement was being worked out to secure Beihl's release in exchange for "lenient treatment" of the Basque terrorists awaiting court-martial sentences.[43] The official Spanish Government news agency confirmed a meeting between members of the Basque E.T.A. and "parties interested" in securing the release of Consul Beihl. The Basque sources indicated a three-step arrangement whereby Beihl would first be freed, the court-martial would then announce its verdicts and sentences, and, thirdly, any death sentences ordered would be commuted by Generalissimo Franco. According to their statements, the prior release of Consul Beihl would allow commutation as an act of clemency rather than as a response to pressure.

West German Consul Beihl was freed on December 25th, 1970, just one day before the verdict of the Burgos court-martial was expected. His release on Christmas Day was regarded as a timed, tactical maneuver

---

[42] Quoted in *ibid.,* December 6, 1970.
[43] Reported in *The Milwaukee Journal,* December 22, 1970.

with strong emotional and humanitarian overtones. The press speculated that: 1) if no death sentences were now imposed, many Spaniards would wonder why the prisoners and their families had been kept in unnecessary but agonizing suspense over the holidays; 2) if any death sentences were imposed, it would be difficult for the Franco regime to refuse clemency after Beihl's release; or 3) if the Government decided that none of the Burgos defendants should die, any credit it might hope to glean from world public opinion would be overshadowed by the fact that the Basques had made their gesture first.[44] In its own statement, the E.T.A. said the release of Beihl was designed to show the Spanish people and the world that the E.T.A. was not "an irresponsible, fanatical and bloodthirsty band." [45] It warned, however, that if any death sentences were imposed, it would take immediate reprisals.

Although the final verdict was postponed for a few days, when announced it was more severe than had been expected; six Basques were given the death sentence and the other nine were sentenced to long terms of imprisonment. The court-martial stated that it had been proved that the E.T.A. was a "separatist-Marxist-terrorist organization . . . whose purposes were to disturb public order, hurt the prestige of the Spanish nation and institutions, destroy by violence the organization of the state, [and] dismember a part of the national territory by subversive actions, terrorism, armed warfare and social revolution." [46] The sentence provoked expressions of shock and pleas for clemency from throughout Europe, and reaction in the Northern Basque provinces of Spain was expected to be so severe that a number of preventive arrests were reported to have been made in the area. In addition, only two days later President Franco commuted all of the death sentences which had been imposed by the court to thirty-year prison terms.[47] This alleviated, temporarily at least, the civil tension throughout Spain and the most serious political crisis which Franco had faced in thirty years.

Because details of the alleged "bargain" between the E.T.A. and the central Government have not been published and the bargain itself remains speculative at best, it is difficult to categorize the Beihl diplonapping in any definitive sense. If one regards the ransom demands of the E.T.A. to have been prevention of a verdict of the death sentence as

---

[44] *New York Times,* December 26, 1970.
[45] Quoted in *ibid.*
[46] Quoted in *ibid.,* December 29, 1970. (Parenthetical insert added.)
[47] *Ibid.,* December 31, 1970.

was originally reported, then obviously those demands were not acceded to. If, however, the principal aim of the Basques was to prevent the actual imposition of the death sentence by securing its commutation, then they were successful. Nonetheless, the Franco Government clearly did not publicly accede to any demands *in advance* and although the death sentence was ultimately commuted, the commutation followed Beihl's release and therefore could not technically be regarded as ransom for it. Moreover, it remains unclear whether Generalissimo Franco actually commuted the death sentence because of a secret deal with the E.T.A., because of the dangers of more widespread internal turmoil, or because of the world-wide public furor which had arisen in response to the Burgos court-martial and the verdicts reached. The Beihl case may well epitomize a diplonapping with "no ransom"—but ultimate success for the kidnappers' objectives.

The two final case studies of Category Three kidnappings in which demands were not met (or made) but the victims were released unharmed took place in Turkey in February and March, 1971. Since both involved the abduction of American servicemen they cannot be considered actual "diplonappings." However, because they did not occur in Latin America but their pattern of execution and apparent objectives were nevertheless similar to the diplomatic kidnappings already examined, they would seem to merit brief inclusion here for purposes of comparison and contrast. In February, three armed Turkish extremists kidnapped a U.S. Air Force enlisted man, James Finley, on the outskirts of Ankara, Turkey.[48] The American Embassy in Ankara asked the Turkish Foreign Ministry to do everything possible to secure his safe return. Although the kidnappers' identities were not uncovered, they appeared to be motivated more by the anti-American sentiment then virulent in Turkey than by any desire to strike a ransom bargain; no demands for money or for the release of any prisoners were publicly made. After being held captive for approximately seventeen hours, the U.S. serviceman was freed unharmed. No details regarding his release or his report on the kidnapping were published.

The second Turkish kidnapping provides more of a parallel to some of its Latin American predecessors in that ransom was specifically demanded. In March, 1971, four U.S. Air Force servicemen were kidnapped by five armed terrorists who demanded $400,000 in ransom

---

[48] *The Milwaukee Journal,* February 15-16, 1971.

and threatened to put the kidnapped airmen in front of a "firing squad" if the money was not paid.[49] The ransom note came from the Turkish People's Liberation Army, a revolutionary group which also claimed responsibility for the February kidnapping of Sgt. Finley; it called on Turks to revolt against the Turkish "conservative government" and end Turkish membership in NATO. The United States Ambassador to Turkey stated that he was in touch with the Turkish Foreign Ministry and security officials but an Embassy spokesman said that no decision regarding the payment of the ransom had been taken. At a White House news conference President Nixon stated that he "would not suggest that the Turkish government negotiate" with the kidnappers.[50]

Following the kidnapping, thousands of policemen and troops initiated a search for the airmen. Riots and fighting broke out at the Middle East Technical University in Ankara when troops attempted to search a university dormitory for the kidnapped men; at least twelve soldiers and students were hurt and one student and soldier were killed in the ensuing gunfight. The Turkish Government indicated that it had mobilized 30,000 troops and police for the search, that 356 persons had been detained for questioning, and that 26 others had been arrested in connection with the kidnappings. Many of those detained were suspected of having received their military and political training from the Palestinian guerillas. Meanwhile, the Turkish Government publicly refused to accede to the kidnappers' ransom demands. After a Turkish cabinet meeting, the Labor Minister stated, "You don't bargain with bandits." [51] As in the Mitrione and Fly diplonappings involving kidnapped Americans in Uruguay, the U.S. Government refused to apply any pressure on Turkey to negotiate and simply appealed to the kidnappers directly to free the four men.

Finally, on March 8, 1971, the Turkish guerillas freed the four kidnapped hostages by simply leaving them in an unguarded apartment only 700 yards away from the U.S. Embassy in Ankara. Turkish officials said that the kidnappers had phoned acquaintances several times on the 8th in attempts to get rid of their captives; apparently unsuccessful, they left the airmen alone late that evening in the apartment where they had been held since their abduction. The four released

---

[49] The following account has been drawn largely from *The Milwaukee Journal*, March 4-9, 1971.

[50] Quoted in *ibid.*, March 5 and 6, 1971.

[51] *Ibid.*, March 6, 1971.

men were questioned immediately by both American officials and Turkish police but their statements were not made public. However, at a press conference in Ankara one of the men stated that the kidnappers had said that the airmen had been kidnapped because the rebels wanted to "liberate Turkey," but no other information was given. U.S. Secretary of State Rogers thanked the Turkish Government for its "vigorous and extraordinary efforts" to free the American servicemen.[52]

Both Turkish and U.S. officials maintained that no ransom had been paid to the kidnappers and State Department officials once again indicated that the payment of ransom had been ruled out by the United States because it would encourage other kidnappings. As will be seen in Chapters VI and VIII, the United States Government had gradually come to the conclusion that a policy of minimizing the rewards—partly by refusing to accede to ransom demands and partly by refusing political asylum to any released prisoners—would help contribute to an overall preventive strategy of discouraging all diplomatic kidnappings in the future. Unfortunately, only the Argentine case involving the Paraguayan Consul and the Turkish kidnapping of the four U.S. airmen have provided clear-cut examples of successful policies of "no ransom" in which the hostages were released despite the adamant refusal of the governments concerned to accede to the kidnappers' demands.

Two recent "quasi-kidnappings" which allegedly occurred in Africa and in the Middle East afford rather uncertain examples for either the second or third categories of diplomappings mentioned since so little is known about them at the present time. They may or may not have been cases in which the demands made were actually answered and the African case, in fact, may have been an elaborate hoax. In Uganda, a first secretary at the British High Commission in Kampala, Brian A. Lea,[53] was allegedly kidnapped in early May, 1970; a phone informant with news of the abduction reportedly asked no ransom and gave no reason for the "kidnapping." Although police launched an immediate search, Lea was not found until the next day when he appeared, apparently released. No details of the case were given at the time, including no mention of how or where Lea was found. The London Times reported that the British High Commission had ordered Lea to keep silent

[52] Ibid., March 9, 1971.
[53] Case reported in the New York Times, May 4 and 5, 1970, in The Milwaukee Journal, May 5, 1970, and in the London Times, May 4, 5, 6, 9, and 10, 1970.

about the kidnapping; both Lea and his wife were instructed to stay at home and to make no further statement to the press.[54]

Press speculation on the reasons for the supposed kidnapping centered on Lea's involvement as first secretary for administration and consular affairs in refusing British entry vouchers to East African Asians who hold British passports; a protest against British immigration laws had taken place at the British passport office in Kampala on March 10. In contrast, Uganda's President Obote stated firmly that his government was convinced that Lea was not kidnapped and set up an official inquiry into the whole matter. Meanwhile, the British Foreign Office stated that Lea was being recalled; it was not announced whether or not he would give evidence in the Ugandan inquiry. The results of the inquiry were not available at the time of writing this account but subsequent press reports indicated that Lea had probably never been kidnapped at all but had gone into voluntary hiding on a small island on Lake Victoria. Rumors of his involvement in an illicit affair made the entire episode intriguing, but less than relevant for the purposes of this analysis.

The kidnapping of an American diplomat, Morris Draper,[55] by Palestinian Arab commandos in Jordan in June, 1970, was more similar in nature to the Latin American diplonappings and was apparently the first of its kind in the Middle East. Draper, head of the political section of the American Embassy in Amman, was kidnapped one evening and released the following day; a U.S. Embassy spokesman gave no details of how or when Draper was released. Before his release, Draper's diplonapping was reportedly discussed at a Jordanian Cabinet meeting as well as at a meeting of high officials presided over by King Hussein; the acting head of the American Embassy had reported to the State Department that the Jordanian Government had indicated that Draper "might be released soon." According to press reports, the commandos had been seeking the release of forty guerillas held by the Jordanian Government in trade for Draper and it was believed that the agreement to free him was reached following contacts between the Jordanian Government and the commandos. Whether or not the guerilla prisoners were in fact set free was not reported and after his release Draper's own whereabouts were not disclosed by the U.S. Embassy. The entire matter remained somewhat of a mystery in terms of the published account,

[54] *London Times,* May 6, 1970.
[55] The Draper account is based on reports in the *New York Times,* June 9 and 10, 1970, and in *The Milwaukee Journal,* June 8, 1970.

and the terse statements of the United States and Jordanian governments did not help to clarify it.

In conclusion, it is evident that the largest number of diplonapping cases have arisen in Category Two—kidnappings in which the political prisoners demanded were released or the ransom asked for was paid and the kidnapped diplomats were subsequently freed unharmed. These, in other words, were the "successful" diplonappings (from the point of view of the diplonappers themselves), both in terms of motivations satisfied and in terms of results attained. Only a few cases of kidnapping attempts which were foiled before completion have been cited, although it is admitted that there may have been other cases which have not been publicized or which might have escaped attention in this survey.

Finally, the most notable examples (and perhaps the only ones) of Category Three—cases in which the demands made were not acceded to and the kidnapped hostages were nonetheless freed—were the recent diplonapping of the Paraguayan consul in Argentina and the kidnapping of the four American airmen in Turkey. Despite the refusal of Argentina to release the political prisoners requested and of Turkey to pay the ransom demanded, the hostages were released in both cases. At cursory glance, it might be argued that this is the way to deal with such terrorism—simply to refuse to bow to it and to hope that humanitarian considerations will prevent the actual execution of the threats made. The diplonappings examined in Chapter VI make it quite clear, however, that such sentiments do not always prevail, and that the threats of reprisal, including murder, must be taken seriously.

LATIN AMERICAN KIDNAPPINGS:
ASSASSINATIONS AND TERRORISM

Chapter V has examined several cases of "successful" diplonappings in which the kidnappers' demands were fully met, a few situations in which apparent kidnapping attempts were made and failed, and at least two cases of kidnappings in which the hostages were released even though the host governments did not accede to the kidnappers' demands. Despite the latter, two recent cases have demonstrated dramatically the dangers inherent in no-ransom policies pursued in a political milieu of revolution and terrorism. It is essential to recognize that the effectiveness of diplonapping as a terrorist weapon is dependent upon an atmosphere of political turmoil and an attitude of psychological doubt. If the governments concerned could predict the exact reaction of terrorist groups to a refusal to accept their terms, the uncertainty which has frequently led to submission would be removed. The authorities could then respond either to the reality of the threat or to its emptiness and react accordingly. Unfortunately, that element of uncertainty has been increased, rather than lessened, by the von Spreti and Mitrione murders in Guatemala and Uruguay respectively in 1970.

Guatemala has provided the uneasy setting for revolutionary and terrorist activities for several years. Thus, a veritable series of political kidnappings took place both in 1965 and in 1966 and, as has been mentioned above, the United States Ambassador to Guatemala was assassinated in August, 1968, in an abortive kidnapping attempt. Earlier that same year, in January, two United States military attachés at the American Embassy in Guatemala were shot to death in a terrorist attack.[1] Although it was not immediately clear whether the murders were the result of a random attack or aimed directly at United States personnel, the Rebel Armed Forces (a major Communist group in

---

[1] Account based on reports in the *New York Times,* January 17 and 18, 1968.

Guatemala which subsequently announced that it was responsible for the slayings) stated that they were specifically aimed at the American mission in Guatemala which, they charged, had participated in the organization of "killer" teams by the Guatemalan Army. Following the attack, the Guatemalan Government proclaimed a "state of alarm" or modified martial law and the United States Embassy was placed under special guard. United States officials stated that they had no intention of lodging a formal protest to the Guatemalan Government about the assassinations.

In addition to such acts of outright terrorism, the precedent-setting kidnapping of a Roman Catholic prelate took place in March, 1968, when Archbishop Mario Casariego of Guatemala was kidnapped in his car *en route* to his residence.[2] Although the Rebel Armed Forces reportedly disclaimed any involvement in this kidnapping, the Government of Guatemala immediately proclaimed a state of siege and decreed an effective take-over of the country by the armed forces; all police forces were placed under the direct military command of the Defense Department, all political activity was suspended, and security forces were granted the right of search and seizure without judicial warrants. Doubts gradually emerged as to whether the kidnappers represented the far left or the far right, however, and the *New York Times* reported that "informed persons" appeared inclined to accept the denials of the leftist F.A.R. (Rebel Armed Forces) at face value and to look instead to the extreme right for the kidnappers.

After a few days the Archbishop was released unharmed and the chief of the Guatemalan police subsequently identified the kidnappers as leaders of an ultra-rightist conspiracy designed to overthrow the President. It was believed that they had hoped to split the Guatemalan Government from the Church and the Army but that when church leaders publicly supported the President, and the Army showed no dissidence, they had abandoned their plot. Although this abduction of the Archbishop was not a "diplonapping" in the sense of involving a foreign diplomat, it did provide a highly-publicized precedent in its attempt to influence the policies or affect the power of the government concerned. It showed, even in its failure, the degree of publicity and official concern that a small group of terrorists could create by the kidnapping of a public figure of some renown.

---

[2] Account based on reports in the *New York Times,* March 18-22, 1968.

Another Guatemalan kidnapping which provided a more immediate precedent for the von Spreti affair occurred in February, 1970, when the Rebel Armed Forces kidnapped the Foreign Minister of Guatemala, Alberto Fuentes Mohr.[3] The F.A.R. gave the Government 24 hours to free a university student who had been arrested as a member of a terrorist organization and to grant him access to the Mexican Embassy in exchange for the release of Mohr. In this case the Government acceded to their demand and freed the student who was granted political asylum in the residence of the Mexican Ambassador. Foreign Minister Mohr was then released after his captors called a local newspaper and arranged to deliver him to its offices. This kidnapping took place against the background of a national election which had created nation-wide apprehension and concern even though the election itself turned out to be a relatively peaceful one. It preceded by only one month the diplonapping of the West German Ambassador to Guatemala, Count Karl von Spreti.

Ambassador von Spreti was kidnapped by terrorists on March 31st, 1970.[4] According to news reports, he was seized while in his own car outside his residence, having left the German Embassy shortly after noon. Guatemalan officials stated that they presumed that the kidnapping had been carried out by the Rebel Armed Forces, the urban guerillas responsible for much of the recent terrorism in Guatemala. The following day this assumption was confirmed when the Ambassador sent a personal note which was dropped in the mailbox of the West German Chargé d'Affaires and which stated: "I am in the hands of the F.A.R. I am feeling well and expect to be returned soon." [5] The Guatemalan Foreign Ministry gave assurances to the Government of the German Federal Republic that it would do everything in its power to obtain Ambassador von Spreti's safe return. In addition, it was announced that the Papal Nuncio, dean of the diplomatic corps in Guatemala, was in contact with both the Guatemalan Government and the West German Embassy, presumably acting as an intermediary between them in the entire matter.

It was therefore with some surprise and a sense of shock that the world learned of the refusal of the Guatemalan Government to accept the conditions and demands of the guerillas for the release of the Am-

[3] Account based on reports in the *New York Times,* February 28 and March 1 and 2, 1970.
[4] Account based on reports in the *New York Times,* April 1-7, 1970.
[5] *New York Times,* April 2, 1970.

bassador. The original communication only specified the release of seventeen political prisoners in return for von Spreti's freedom; it did not include a demand for monetary ransom. In its rejection of these terms, the Government announced that it found it "...impossible *legally* to accede to the demands of the kidnappers..." [6] It argued that some of the seventeen political prisoners who had been designated by the F.A.R. were "convicted criminals" and could not be freed by executive orders. In letters to the Government and to the Papal Nuncio, the diplonappers had threatened "to execute" von Spreti unless the political prisoners were freed; on the basis of that threat a West German Embassy official said of the Guatemalan Government's refusal: "They have sentenced him to death." [7] Unfortunately, he was proven to be tragically right in his prediction.

Following the Government's announcement that it could not free any of the political prisoners, the terrorists raised their demands for the release of von Spreti to $700,000 in ransom money and freedom for twenty-two political prisoners.[8] What their motivation was in doing so is not clear. It is possible, however, that the diplonappers believed that external pressures, not only from the West German Government and Embassy but also from the other diplomatic missions in Guatemala, would persuade the Guatemalan Government to modify its position and ultimately to accede to their demands. Therefore, they might as well "up the ante." It is quite clear even from the public record that such diplomatic pressures were applied. In Bonn, for example, the Government of the Federal Republic of Germany stated that West Germany did not see itself in a position "to accept the decision" of Guatemala to refuse to exchange the political prisoners for the Ambassador. The West German Government also stated that it was "disappointed" with the lack of action by the Guatemalan Government and sent a special envoy to Guatemala to press its case.

In addition to the German protest, a delegation of several foreign ambassadors stationed in Guatemala met with the Guatemalan Foreign Minister to register their protest against the Government's decision not

[6] *Ibid.*, April 3, 1970. (Italics added.)

[7] *Ibid.*

[8] There are two contradictory statements as to the exact number of political prisoners designated. The *New York Times* issue of April 4 refers to twenty-five prisoners but the issues of April 5 and 12 specify twenty-two. All accounts agree as to the addition of $700,000 in ransom, however.

to meet the kidnappers' demands. Although the Guatemalan Government had issued a general "declaration of war" against the rebel movements, had imposed a state of martial law, and had declared a national state of emergency, the prevailing climate of revolutionary terrorism was so great that the delegation of ambassadors also requested increased physical protection for themselves and their staffs. The danger that the diplonappings could spread elsewhere was also widely recognized. In Venezuela, for example, the police and intelligence chiefs agreed to intensify their own security measures to prevent kidnappings and stated that not only would foreign embassies and diplomatic residences in Caracas be placed under constant vigilance, but foreign ambassadors and other diplomatic personnel would be provided with security guards.[9]

The refusal of the Guatemalan Government to release the political prisoners came under such widespread attack and criticism, particularly after the murder of Ambassador von Spreti, that it deserves more detailed examination at this point. The Guatemalan position was based both on legal argumentation and on political expediency. Legally, it was argued that Guatemalan law prohibited the granting of amnesty for *convicted* prisoners without the approval of the national judiciary. The judiciary apparently was considered to be opposed to any such action. It should be noted that in the kidnapping of Guatemalan Foreign Minister Mohr just one month before, the Government had freed the student demanded in exchange for Mohr's release. In that case, however, the student had only been arrested the preceding day and evidently no judicial procedures had been instituted against him prior to his release. In the von Spreti case, the President stated later that it would have been "unconstitutional" to release the prisoners since they had been already tried and sentenced. Despite these legal impediments, however, the *New York Times* stated that under the new emergency laws, the President could grant amnesty to at least some of the designated prisoners simply by Presidential decree.[10]

The argument based on political expediency perhaps weighed even more heavily in the President's decision to refuse to bow to the terrorist threats. After a campaign in which "law and order" had been stressed in an atmosphere of extreme political unrest, the President had been elected only one month prior to the von Spreti affair. It was clear from

---

[9] *New York Times,* April 7, 1970.
[10] *Ibid.,* April 4, 1970.

all accounts that public opinion supported his rejection of the payment of ransom money and the release of the twenty-two jailed rebels.[11] Therefore, although it was recognized that serious diplomatic repercussions might arise if von Spreti were in fact harmed, the fact that the Government's firm stand against all concessions had been praised locally was regarded as more significant in terms of the domestic political situation. The Guatemalan Army chief of public relations made this clear when he stated that if the President made any concessions at that point chaos would result and the public would not believe in his capacity to remain in office. Moreover, an element of gamble may also have entered into the picture in that when Guatemalan Archbishop Casariego had been kidnapped in 1968 and the public had supported the Government's refusal to bargain at that time, the kidnappers had ultimately conceded and had released the Archbishop unharmed. It is possible that the Government believed that a parallel stance would produce a similar result.

To counteract this reasoning, the West German special envoy to Guatemala, Wilhelm Hoppe, conferred with the President of Guatemala in an attempt to find some compromise solution which would allow the release of Ambassador von Spreti. He reportedly was trying to persuade the Guatemalan Government somehow to modify or soften its rejection of the kidnappers' demands in order to widen the possible options for a deal on the Ambassador's release. Diplomatic pressures from other sources also were aimed at persuading the President to negotiate with the diplonappers. However, by April 5th it was quite clear that the Government would not alter its decision to refuse to meet the ransom demands. The Army public relations chief stated: "The Government will stick to its decision no matter what the cost." [12] The cost was high. Count Karl von Spreti was shot to death by his kidnappers sometime during the night of April 5th.

Following Ambassador von Spreti's murder, the Federal Republic of Germany moved immediately to reduce its diplomatic ties with Guatemala to a minimum.[13] West German Foreign Minister Walter Scheel recalled the acting chief of the German mission in Guatemala as well as most of the mission aides. Moreover, the Guatemalan Ambassador to the Federal Republic in Bonn was "politely" informed that it would

---

[11] *Ibid.,* April 5, 1970.
[12] Quoted in the *New York Times,* April 6, 1970.
[13] *New York Times,* April 7, 1970.

be desirable for him to leave the country. Although Guatemalan army patrols began a house to house search of the capital on April 6th and the Government continued its state of siege, the Federal Republic was not mollified by such action. At a news conference in Bonn the West German Foreign Minister stated that the magnitude of the crime and its occurrence as part of a sequence of "raw force and acts of terrorism in many parts of the world" compelled the Federal Republic of Germany to call on friendly governments for *international* measures to improve the protection of diplomats abroad. He stated, "These events impinge on the foundations of international cooperation." [14]

The West German position implicitly recognized diplomatic inviolability and its protection as basic to the conduct of international diplomacy and explicitly regarded the diplonappings not only as political problems but as legal problems within the context of international law. In his remarks, the Foreign Minister thus emphasized the neglect of a dual obligation on the part of the Guatemalan Government; Bonn regretted both the Guatemalan Government's failure to obtain the Ambassador's release, once kidnapped, and its initial failure to provide adequate protection for him. Since Guatemala was evidently not in a position to provide the protection required by international law, the Foreign Minister concluded, the Federal Republic was recalling its chief of mission. A few days later, having flown to Guatemala to escort Ambassador von Spreti's body back to Germany, Foreign Minister Walter Scheel delivered a final stiff protest to the Guatemalan Government, charging that it had not found itself "in a position to protect the highest German representative and save his life." [15] The fact that the President of Guatemala had ordered state honors to be accorded to Ambassador von Spreti did not greatly affect the German attitude.

A few preliminary observations on the von Spreti diplonapping may be ventured at this point. First, it differed from the vast majority of the other kidnappings in Latin America in that, with the exception of the 1969 Swiss diplonapping in Colombia, it was the first which included a demand for money in ransom. Although the $700,000 ransom demand was added to the original conditions set by the F.A.R., it presents a troublesome precedent: in monetary terms, what is the life of a diplomat worth? It is one decision to refuse to release political

[14] Quoted in *ibid.*
[15] Quoted in the *New York Times,* April 12, 1970.

prisoners on legal or political grounds; it is quite another to refuse to pay a requested amount of money in exchange for a human life. Secondly, the von Spreti case was the first diplonapping which resulted in the murder of the diplomat concerned. Although Guatemala did not set a precedent in its refusal to accede to the diplonappers' demands (Argentina had done so successfully just the previous month), it was the first government to have its refusal answered by such brutal reprisals. Finally, the statements of the Government of the Federal Republic of Germany removed the entire problem of the diplonappings from the realm of newspapers headlines to the realm of international law and politics. The terrorist technique of diplonapping—and the life and death magnitude of its success or failure—has presented an entirely new, complex, and extremely delicate problem for the continued conduct and operations of world diplomacy.

The second case study in Category Four—kidnappings in which governmental refusals to accede to kidnapper demands resulted in the assassination of the kidnapped diplomats—occurred in Uruguay in 1970. This was the highly publicized diplonapping of Dan A. Mitrione, a United States A.I.D. advisor to the Uruguayan police force. As in the von Spreti case, the details of the kidnapping and the policies pursued by the various governments involved can best be understood in the context of the popular unrest, student rioting, and sporadic terrorism which prevailed in Uruguay, much as it did in Guatemala, throughout the late 1960's. The Mitrione diplonapping can not be regarded as a single isolated incident, then, but rather as another link in a chain of events based on the political instability, revolutionary protest, and governmental weakness which characterize several of the regimes of the Latin American republics today.

In Uruguay, the revolutionary movement has been led by the Tupamaros, an urban guerilla group which has rejected elections and is committed to the idea that within Latin America only armed revolution can produce social and economic change. Operating in a country which has been governed by only two political parties for over a century, the Tupamaros were bolstered by the economic slump which hit Uruguay when the world market for its principal exports contracted severely in 1953 and the gross national product declined by about 15 % over a period of twelve years. The resulting economic and social unrest and widespread political discontent were portrayed simply by Carlos Quijano, the director of the respected leftist weekly *Marcha*: "The truth is that people are absolutely fed up with the traditional parties, the traditional way and the government." [16] In opposition to "the traditional way," the Tupamaros have partly armed their movement through thefts and bank robberies and in the late 1960's turned to such terrorist tactics as bombings and kidnappings.

In August, 1968, for example, a leading advisor to the President of Uruguay was kidnapped outside his seaside home by four or five terrorists armed with submachine guns;[17] both his chauffeur and secretary were wounded in the attack. In an intensive search for him, police mounted raids on the University of the Republic in Montevideo where several clashes broke out with students who protested at the raids. The police stated that the raids had been ordered because they had received information pointing to university involvement and because university material was being used for the promotion of violence. A newspaper, El Diario, was subsequently closed down by the Government for "publishing information violating state siege regulations" which had included a ban on information about student rioting; all radio stations were also cautioned against broadcasting news of any disorders, except news released by the Government. After four days the Presidential aide was released in downtown Montevideo and the search for him by approximately 3,000 policemen was called off. The kidnappers, reportedly members of the Tupamaro urban guerilla group, claimed they had "arrested" the advisor for having urged the President toward a tough line during recent labor unrest.

The Tupamaros were also responsible for the kidnapping of a banker and newspaper publisher, Gaetano Pelligrini Giampetro, in September, 1969.[18] In a radio broadcast the day after the kidnapping the Tupamaros demanded a favorable settlement with striking Uruguayan bank workers in exchange for Pelligrini's freedom. They also stated that his life was in danger if any street demonstrators were killed by police. In fact, the strike was settled by coincidence and not as a result of the threat before the specified deadline elapsed, but Pelligrini was still not released. The Tupamaros were apparently dissatisfied because although the strike had ended many of the strikers would be subject to military punishment for having failed to comply with a mobilization decree. It was not until November, some 73 days later, that Pelligrini was finally freed after

[16] Quoted by Joseph Novitski, "Uruguay as a Laboratory for Cuban, Chilean Ideas" in The Milwaukee Journal, January 31, 1971.

[17] Account based on reports in the New York Times, August 8, 10, and 12, 1968.

[18] New York Times, September 8, 1969.

the payment of $ 60,000 as a donation to a Montevideo hospital for city workers.[19]

Although neither of these two cases actually involved the kidnapping of a foreign diplomat, they did illustrate the underlying presence of terrorism both as a latent and as an explicit force in Uruguayan politics during this period. Moreover, they clearly pointed to the importance of the guerilla organization, the Tupamaros, as a well-organized terrorist group with both strength and influence, particularly in urban areas. It was not particularly surprising to the politically astute, then, when the Tupamaros kidnapped the chief United States advisor to the Uruguayan police force on July 31st, 1970;[20] the advisor, Dan A. Mitrione, reportedly knew more about the Tupamaro operations in Uruguay than any other U.S. official. The Tupamaros also attempted, but failed, to kidnap two other U.S. Embassy officials, a second secretary and a cultural affairs officer, in a well-coordinated plan in which each attempt was carried out separately, but synchronized with the others. They succeeded, however, in a fourth attempt with the abduction of a Brazilian consul, Aloysio Mares Diás Gomide, moments after the Mitrione diplonapping. Although no ransom demands were immediately made, it was anticipated that the two men might be bargained in exchange for the release of some political prisoners, since the Uruguayan Government was believed to be holding an estimated 100 to 150 Tupamaros as prisoners.

The Uruguayan Government immediately established a dragnet of police and soldiers around Montevideo and began a thorough search for the two diplomats. This seemed particularly urgent because Mitrione was wounded in the abduction and the Tupamaros stated that they had performed surgery on him. The guerilla demands were finally set forth in a statement to the newspaper *El Diario* in which they asked for the release of all political prisoners as ransom for Mitrione and Diás Gomide; they also instructed that the prisoners, if freed, should be sent to Mexico, Peru, or Algeria. The Government had stated repeatedly that it would not negotiate with the Tupamaros "under any conditions" and President Jorge Pacheco Areco maintained his position "never to negotiate with criminals." However, the press reported that a high official source had hinted that although the President would reject the

[19] *Ibid.*, November 22, 1969.

[20] The following account is based largely on reports in the *New York Times*, August 1-15, 1970, and in *The Milwaukee Journal*, August 1-11, 1970.

specific guerilla demands, he might grant a "general amnesty" for all political prisoners.[21]

Meanwhile, the police continued their nation-wide search for the guerillas and arrested over one hundred suspects. Following an anonymous telephone tip, the police found letters from the two kidnapped men to their wives which stated that they were "in good condition." Mitrione, however, wrote that the Tupamaros were questioning him extensively about his work as advisor to the Uruguayan police; he asked his wife to tell the United States Ambassador, Charles W. Adair, Jr., to "do all he can to free me as soon as possible."[22] The U.S. State Department appealed to the kidnappers to let Mitrione have hospital care for his wound which might otherwise endanger his life.

The position of the Uruguayan Government remained ambivalent. In a communiqué issued by the Ministry of the Interior, the Government indicated that although it was not then ready to negotiate with the Tupamaros, it did not reject the idea of possible future negotiations. The Government also attempted to distinguish between political prisoners and the Tupamaros which it refused to recognize as a legitimate political group. Thus, it stated that the term "political prisoners" did not apply to the more than one hundred imprisoned Tupamaros whom it regarded as "common criminals." Chapter IV pointed out that this distinction between political and common criminals is clearly recognized in international law and is frequently utilized in decisions regarding such things as asylum and/or extradition proceedings. The problem, of course, is to make the determination in practice as to which are which.

On August 5th the Tupamaros announced in a direct message to President Pacheco Areco [23] that they would accept nothing less than the release of *all* political prisoners in exchange for their American and Brazilian hostages; they were not prepared to negotiate on any other points. They also stated that if the prisoners were not released, both Mitrione and Diás Gomide would be submitted "to justice." During this entire period the Governments of both Brazil and the United States were in close and continual contact with the Government of Uruguay

---

[21] *New York Times,* August 3, 1970. How such an amnesty would differ in detail from the guerilla demands was not clear. It can only be assumed that the differences would arise out of conflicting definitions of "political prisoners."

[22] Quoted in *The Milwaukee Journal,* August 3, 1970.

[23] The message was delivered to the President by a Uruguayan Judge who had been kidnapped by the Tupamaros just prior to the Mitrione and Diás Gomide diplonappings; he was released after a week's captivity.

and it was generally assumed that they were urging Uruguay to negotiate. At this point, however, their concern mounted and it was openly reported that Brazil had placed "heavy diplomatic pressure" on Uruguay in an attempt to persuade its Government to ransom the hostages. Despite such pressures, the President refused to negotiate with the Tupamaros and denounced their demands as "extortion against the lawfully constituted government."

On August 8th a communiqué, purportedly from the Tupamaros and distributed to various Uruguayan radio stations, stated that Mitrione would be executed the following noon because of the Government's refusal to release the political prisoners as ransom for him. Although Uruguayan police denied any knowledge of such a message and doubted its authenticity, events proved it to be in earnest. The following day, August 9th, a phone call to radio station *Carve* stated that the urban guerillas had shot and killed Dan Mitrione at noon. The radio station quoted the Tupamaro caller as saying, "In the face of the president of the republic's failure to fulfill the demands of the movement, Mr. Dan Mitrione was executed." [24] The caller stated that Diás Gomide and Claude L. Fly (a U.S. soil expert employed by the Uruguayan Government and kidnapped on August 7) [25] would also be executed if the Government refused to meet their ransom demands. Police again stated they had received no direct communication from the Tupamaros, but they immediately arrested scores of Tupamaro suspects, including some of their top leaders.

Prior to the August 9th announcement of Mitrione's death, a number of last minute attempts to save his life had been made. Just twenty minutes before the noon deadline, the United States Ambassador to Uruguay, Charles W. Adair, Jr., broadcast a final appeal for mercy over Uruguayan radio stations:

The violent assassination of this man, an innocent victim of circumstances, would be a high crime not only against the traditions of western society, but also against humanity.[26]

Ambassador Adair made this appeal after having met with the Uruguayan Foreign Minister. However, the Government of Uruguay did not give either the United States or Brazil much hope of saving any of the three

---

[24] Quoted in *The Milwaukee Sentinel,* August 10, 1970.
[25] See below, pp. 107-109.
[26] Quoted in *The Milwaukee Sentinel,* August 10, 1970.

hostages. A Foreign Ministry spokesman stated that Uruguay had adopted a "realistic" position and did not hide the seriousness of the situation. The Brazilian Government, having freed several political prisoners of its own in exchange for the release of both Ambassador Elbrick in September, 1969, and Ambassador von Holleben in June, 1970, was in a particularly strong position to urge the release of the prisoners in exchange for the freedom of Diás Gomide. Uruguay itself attempted to avert the impending disaster by a series of moves which culminated in a street by street search by 5,000 armed police and soldiers in Montevideo and the arrest of over 100 persons for questioning. Finally, three public Uruguayan figures of some note offered themselves as hostages for the release of Mitrione, Diás Gomide, and Fly—all to no avail.

The dead body of Dan Mitrios was found in a car on a residential street in Montevideo on August 10th; he had been shot in the head twice, apparently early that morning. Uruguayan President Pacheco Areco described the murder as "the greatest attack this country's political institutions have faced in this century" [27] and expressed his personal sympathy to the Mitrione family. The Uruguayan President also requested and received congressional approval of a bill suspending several civil rights and granting him sweeping dictatorial powers to fight the Tupamaros. Nonetheless, the President's refusal to answer the guerilla demands or even to negotiate with them came under attack from an increasingly large group within the country itself. Moreover, a number of Uruguayan congressmen were advocating and pressing for the establishment of the death penalty for terrorists. In Brazil, there was also strong criticism of the Uruguayan President's refusal to negotiate with the Tupamaros. Washington, however, (though having urged Uruguay to do "all possible" to save Mitrione's life and having condemned "the essential inhumanity of the terrorists") was not directly critical of the Government of Uruguay for its position not to accede to the ransom demands.

Following the murder of Mitrione, the Uruguayan Government issued a formal statement explaining and defending its decision not to negotiate with the diplonappers nor to accede to their demands as follows:

It is not legally possible, honorable or conducive to anything for the government to negotiate with criminal organizations—even when acting with the noble aim of saving precious and innocent lives...[28]

[27] Quoted in the *New York Times,* August 11, 1970.
[28] Quoted in *The Milwaukee Journal,* August 11, 1970.

This contention re-emphasized their view that there was a clear distinction between political prisoners and common criminals which could not be overlooked without detriment to the integrity of the government concerned. At the same time, the United States Department of State made it clear that although the U.S. Government had urged the Uruguayan Government to do everything possible to secure Mitrione's safe return, it did *not* press Uruguay to accede to the kidnappers' demands, because such action would encourage other terrorists to attempt to kidnap more Americans in the future.[29] This perhaps unexpected support for the Uruguayan position was the first time the State Department had publicly disclosed some of its own views on the Latin American diplonappings and how best to deal with them. Other suggestions—from the State Department and elsewhere—will be reviewed and analyzed in Chapter VIII.

Meanwhile, the whereabouts of the two other kidnapped diplomats —the Brazilian consul and the U.S. agricultural expert—continued to be unknown. Police denied any new threats from the Tupamaros, but news censorship prevented any accurate assessment of the situation. Over 10,000 troops embarked upon a virtual door to door search for the remaining two hostages, while a combination of student demonstrations and terrorist bombings added fuel to the fires of tension, rumors, and dissension. The search continued despite the Tupamaros' threat to execute Diás Gomide and Fly immediately if their hiding place was discovered. Although the Uruguayan Government seemed to be facing a virtual stalemate in its attempts to find the two men, foreign diplomats stationed in Uruguay were reportedly attempting to devise a plan whereby negotiations with the Tupamaros could take place without interference in the internal affairs of Uruguay.[30] Secret negotiations apparently did follow and in early September it was reported that the Tupamaros might have changed their ransom package. Instead of demanding the release of all political prisoners, they were then supposedly asking for one million dollars in ransom money, publication of a manifesto, and a new trial for nine Tupamaros who had been sentenced to prison the previous week.[31]

One million dollars in ransom were in fact subsequently demanded for the release of Diás Gomide, and in mid-January, 1971, a letter, purportedly from the Tupamaros and sent to Mrs. Fly, specifically

[29] *New York Times,* August 11, 1970.
[30] Reported in *The Milwaukee Journal,* August 23, 1970.
[31] *The Milwaukee Sentinel,* September 8, 1970.

requested one million dollars for Claude Fly's release.[32] Although Fly's son stated that the burden of raising the money should fall on the governments of the United States and Uruguay, the U.S. State Department indicated that the United States had refused to pay any ransom. The Government also opposed its payment by private groups or individuals on the grounds that this would encourage more political kidnappings and ransom demands in the future.[33]

Despite the "no negotiation" stance of the Uruguayan Government and the "no ransom" policy of the United States, both Diás Gomide and Fly were ultimately released in early 1971. The Tupamaros released the Brazilian Consul on February 21st in exchange for reported ransom moneys of between $250,000 and $1,000,000, purportedly paid by Mrs. Diás Gomide.[34] The details of his release were not made public, although he was reportedly in good health. Finally, on March 2nd, the Tupamaro guerillas freed Claude Fly approximately eight or nine days after he had suffered a heart attack.[35] According to all information available, there was no ransom paid. Fly had been in captivity for seven months and wrote a 600-page diary on his life and on his experiences while imprisoned which was released with him when he was freed. The diary had not been published or made public prior to the writing of this account.

Unfortunately for the diplomatic community stationed in Montevideo, the release of Diás Gomide and Claude Fly did not signal the end of the diplonapping rampage of the Uruguayan Tupamaros. In January, 1971, before both their releases, the Tupamaros had kidnapped the British Ambassador to Uruguay four blocks from the British Embassy in downtown Montevideo.[36] Almost in defiance of the no exchange, hard-line policy of Uruguayan President Pacheco Areco, the urban guerillas were apparently seeking to increase their pressure on the Government by adding Ambassador Geoffrey Jackson to the other two hostages already held as potential bargain pawns for the release of jailed terrorists. In a note sent to the Government a few days later the Tupamaros claimed responsibility for the kidnapping but made no specific ransom offer and

[32] *New York Times,* January 16, 1971.

[33] *Ibid.,* January 18, 1971. It was not disclosed just how or when the U.S. Government had received the ransom demand or how it had been rejected.

[34] *New York Times,* February 22, 1971.

[35] *Ibid.,* March 3, 1971.

[36] The following account was reported in *ibid.,* January 9, 1971.

indicated that the Government would have to reopen negotiations. In response, the President asked Congress for a grant of special police powers to search for the kidnappers; these were granted for a period of forty days. The temporary suspension of individual rights empowered more than 12,000 police and troops to search private homes without warrants and to hold arrested suspects without court hearings.[37]

Therefore, despite the release of the Brazilian Consul and U.S. agricultural advisor Claude Fly, the Uruguayan political scene was embroiled in turmoil throughout 1971 and British Ambassador Jackson remained in captivity. In March the Tupamaros kidnapped the Uruguayan Attorney General for "an official talk" and indicated that he was being held in a "people's jail." [38] When released thirteen days later, Attorney General Guido Berro Oribe reported that he had been held in the same place as Ambassador Jackson and that the Ambassador was in good health.[39]

Finally, after eight months of imprisonment in a virtual underground dungeon, Ambassador Jackson was freed in early September with the explanation by his Tupamaro captors that he had been given "amnesty" for the escape of 106 guerilla prisoners just a few days before.[40] The Tupamaros maintained that there was no further need to detain the Ambassador because they had already won their "fight for political prisoners" [41] and that the successful jailbreak had seriously undermined the regime of President Jorge Pacheco Areco who faced an election in late November. The *New York Times* concluded its account of the Jackson diplonapping with the assertion that the guerillas were determined to establish themselves as "a second power, parallel to the state, in Uruguay." [42]

At a press conference held in London shortly after his release, Ambassador Jackson set forth his own view that the Tupamaros were "with certain reservations intelligent" and had moved by kidnapping him into the "diplomatic world of negotiations." [43] Although he stated that this captors had made it quite clear that they would have shot him had the Uruguayan Government forces located their "prison," Ambassador

---

[37] *The Washington Post,* January 12, 1971.
[38] *The Milwaukee Journal,* March 11, 1971.
[39] *Ibid.,* March 25, 1971.
[40] *New York Times,* September 11, 1971.
[41] *The Milwaukee Journal,* September 10, 1971.
[42] *New York Times,* September 11, 1971.
[43] Reported in *The London Times,* September 16, 1971.

Jackson nonetheless expressed his own conviction that the basic strategy of dealing with such guerillas must be to show them that the "business of ambassador snatching is self-defeating." He argued that even if the Tupamaros had killed him, a "law of increasing expendability" would ultimately come into operation and eventually the world community "would have to say 'no'." Such a view reinforces the argument favoring a policy of "no rewards" which will be elaborated upon in more detail in Chapter VIII.

Some tentative conclusions which may be drawn from the Guatemalan and Uruguayan cases strongly support the theses set forth in Chapter I that the diplomatic kidnappings are primarily the tools of urban guerillas who have used them both as political leverage against the governments in power and as terrorist techniques to secure publicity for their cause. Moreover, they derive their effectiveness as political weapons primarily from the fact that they so clearly contravene such well-established principles of international law as diplomatic inviolability, and thus automatically concern the entire diplomatic community as well as the host governments which bear the responsibility for special protection. Finally, they illustrate the importance of an efficiently organized and fairly complex underground network which has been the mark of the urban guerillas in contradistinction to their rural counterparts and predecessors.

Before concluding, a few of the parallels and similarities between the von Spreti and Mitrione cases should be noted. Both diplonappings followed upon a long period of political turmoil and acts of terrorism; the kidnappings were designed, therefore, not only to obtain the release of designated political prisoners, but also to reinforce the image of the terrorists as powerful political forces to be reckoned with. Thus, although both terrorist groups "failed" in not achieving the release of the political prisoners demanded, they "succeeded" in impressing upon the governments concerned—and upon the international community in general—the fact of their own strength and determination. Secondly, both cases involved the murder—or, as the terrorists maintained, "the execution"—of the kidnapped diplomats. This, in itself, made the diplonapping threat more credible, and more dangerous, as a future technique of political terrorism. Finally, in terms of the entire diplomatic community, both diplonappings raised broader questions of international law and national policies which previously had been regarded only sporadically and on a piecemeal basis by the individual states concerned. Diplonapping had indeed come of age as an international problem of growing notoriety.

CHAPTER VII

NORTH AMERICAN COUNTERPARTS:
THE CANADIAN CASES

Although the vast majority of the diplomatic kidnappings have taken place in the unsettled political atmosphere of Latin America, North America has also had to deal with its own counterparts. Of particular note were the abduction of James Cross, a senior British consular officer in Quebec, Canada, and the kidnapping and murder of Pierre Laporte, Quebec's Labor Minister, both of which occurred in October, 1970. The first attempts at diplonapping in North America, these Canadian cases, like their Latin American prototypes, unfolded against a backdrop of political discontent and revolutionary terrorism. Though Laporte, as a Canadian government official, did not actually fit the "diplonapping" category, his abduction was so clearly related to the terrorist technique of utilizing innocent individuals as the tools of political blackmail and persuasion, that his case will be considered here along with that of Cross.

Canadian terrorism emerged out of the partial failure of the so-called "quiet revolution"—the attempt to achieve Quebec independence by peaceful means. As it became increasingly evident to French Canadian separatists that the goal of independence for Quebec would not be reached in the immediate future, if at all, the radicals among them organized into such terrorist groups as "Le Front de Libération du Quebec" (FLQ) and the Popular Liberation Front (FLP). From peaceful protest demonstrations in 1962 and 1963 to sporadic bombings from 1963 to 1966, the extremists proceeded not only to overt actions of terrorism, but also to the development of a revolutionary theory. A 1969 document authored by Charles Gagnon, one of the FLQ's theoreticians, states: "There are not 50 strategies. There are only two: the electoral and the revolutionary. [The FLQ and other movements] rejects the electoral idea. That is, they have opted for a revolutionary overthrow of the established order." [1]

[1] Quoted in *The Milwaukee Journal*, November 11, 1970. Parenthetical summary inserted.

As Chapter I emphasized, this rejection of evolutionary change has appeared as a common theme in the pronouncements of all of the terrorist movements which have been involved in the various diplomatic kidnappings included in this study. Seizing upon violence as the only alternative open to a revolutionary minority, the revolutionaries have regarded terrorism as a political technique aimed at political goals. Thus, according to the FLQ document quoted above: "This first stage in the struggle [for independence] is essentially political. And the bombings which characterize it, as much as the demonstrations, strikes and sporadic occupations, do not form military action against the system but a political activity." [2] So also the diplonappings have been utilized as political tools of the terrorists to achieve not only such immediate objectives as monetary rewards or release of prisoners, but also to help create and maintain an atmosphere of public tension and perhaps even governmental repression in which the second stage of overt military conflict may more easily take place.

The kidnappings of James R. Cross and Pierre Laporte, the events and negotiations which followed upon them, and the subsequent measures taken by the Canadian Government provide an excellent case study of the success and limitations of both the theory and the practice of terrorism as a political technique. The facts surrounding the Cross kidnapping provide a familiar story.[3] On October 5, 1970, four men, three armed with submachine guns, abducted Cross from his home at gunpoint. A note found at the University of Quebec demanded freedom for twenty-three political prisoners, their flight to Cuba or Algeria, and $500,000 for the release of Cross; a 48-hour deadline was set. Because of the note's demand for publication in all Quebec newspapers of the FLQ's political manifesto, it was clear that the kidnapping had been perpetrated by elements of that terrorist organization. A subsequent communication from the kidnappers received on October 6 stated that if their demands were not met within the time limit, " . . . we cannot be responsible for what happens." [4]

Following the kidnapping, the Combined Antiterrorist Squad, a police group specializing in the activities of the French Canadian separatists, immediately began investigations; on the other hand, Montreal police

    [2] *Ibid.*

    [3] The following account is based largely on articles in the *New York Times,* October 6-10, 1970, and *The Milwaukee Journal,* October 5-9, 1970.

    [4] Quoted in the *New York Times,* October 7, 1970.

reportedly halted their public search for the kidnappers when the ransom note indicated that no police action should be taken.[5] The Canadian Government subsequently promised additional protection for all foreign diplomats stationed in Canada. Kidnapping itself is a federal offense in Canada, with a maximum penalty of life imprisonment; however, the first official reaction to the ransom demands appeared uncertain when neither federal nor provincial governments could reach a decision on how to respond to them. The Canadian Foreign Secretary, Mitchell Sharp, summed up the Government's perplexity simply: "We don't know how to deal with it." [6] Although law enforcement in Canada is a provincial responsibility, the Quebec provincial Minister of Justice indicated that any decision would be a joint one by provincial and federal governments.

By October 7th an official position was reached. Foreign Secretary Sharp stated that the Government considered the ransom demands to be wholly unreasonable and would not meet them. However, he invited the kidnappers to establish communications with the Government and asked them to name a representative to negotiate the terms for Cross's release. He also indicated that the Government was prepared to publicize the FLQ separatist manifesto; this was ultimately broadcast on government-owned radio and television. Meanwhile, the original deadline set by the terrorists for the satisfaction of their demands was extended several different times. They stated on one occasion that they were extending the deadline to show their good faith and that " . . . we do not put [the] life of diplomat James Cross in jeopardy for a question of money." [7] However, they later warned the authorities that if their demands were not met, the FLQ would be obliged to "execute" Cross.

During this entire time—the first five days following the diplonapping—the kidnappers thus kept in close communication with the Government and *vice versa*. Although they rejected its initial proposal to designate a representative for purposes of negotiation, they stated that they would continue to establish communications in their own way. It also appeared that they were willing to modify their conditions for the release of Cross. In their statement of October 9th the FLQ again

---

[5] When questioned in the House of Commons regarding this report, Canadian Prime Minister Trudeau indicated that the police may only have "pretended" to halt their search. *Ibid.*

[6] Quoted in *The Milwaukee Journal,* October 6, 1970.

[7] Quoted in the *New York Times,* October 8, 1970.

postponed the set deadline and asked the Government to indicate which of the ransom demands it felt were unreasonable. In addition, the FLQ repeated their demands for the broadcast of their political manifesto and asked the authorities to order the police to stop "their searches, raids, arrests or tortures." [8] As mentioned, the Govenment did comply with the demand for publicity and broadcast the 1400-word statement of the Front over both national radio and television. Government officials were notably silent, however, over which demands they regarded as unreasonable. Moreover, on October 10th the Government asked the kidnappers for fresh proof that James Cross was still alive. A spokesman for both federal and provincial governments asked for a handwritten note from Cross as the required proof that he was still "sound and safe."

It was at this point that the case became obfuscated by the complication of a second kidnapping—the abduction of Quebec's Labor Minister, Mr. Pierre Laporte, from his home on October 10th. Only fifteen minutes prior to the kidnapping, the provincial Quebec government had announced that it would give the Cross kidnappers safe passage out of the country in return for Cross's release, but that it would not release the 23 political prisoners demanded. The government spokesman stated that no society could allow "the decisions of its governmental institutions and courts be put into question or erased by blackmail." [9] Moreover, he stated that the government could not agree to forget crimes already committed. Among the 23 designated prisoners were Front members who had been accused or convicted of armed robbery, involuntary homicide, and conspiracy to kidnap (four were serving life terms and the others sentences of up to 25 years).

After Laporte's abduction, the FLQ ransom demands were reiterated and new deadlines were set on both Cross's and Laporte's lives if the stated stipulations were not met. It soon became evident that two different groups or "cells" of the FLQ were separately involved in the two kidnappings; it was not clear, however, to what extent the two were in collaboration or under joint direction. [10] Quebec's Premier Bourassa rejected the demands on October 11 but broadcast an appeal to the kidnappers to provide proof that both Cross and Laporte were

[8] Quoted in *ibid.*, October 9, 1970.

[9] Quoted in *ibid.*, October 11, 1970.

[10] In an interview after he was ultimately freed James Cross stated that when his kidnappers heard the news on radio that Laporte had been kidnapped this appeared to be "a complete surprise" to them. *The Globe and Mail* (Toronto), December 10, 1970.

still alive and to open negotiations with the government. The following day both cells of FLQ issued statements that they had suspended the deadlines on the lives of both hostages and proposed that an intermediary be agreed upon to initiate and carry on contacts between the Front and the government.[11] Although new deadlines were not set, the cells' statements cautioned that "there are limits to our patience" and the cell which kidnapped Laporte stated in its note to Premier Bourassa that "hesitation on your part will be considered as a tacit refusal and will lead to the execution of Pierre Laporte." [12] Simultaneously, however, a letter from James Cross was released in which the diplomat thanked Bourassa "for saving my life and that of Mr. Laporte." [13]

On October 13 talks began in Montreal between the FLQ's negotiator, Robert Lemieux, and the government's representative, Robert Demers, who had been appointed by Quebec's Premier. The talks took place in the city jail where Lemieux was himself being held at that time on a charge of obstructing justice. Although it first appeared that the negotiations might break down because of a lack of any clear guidelines to Lemieux from the FLQ, a joint communiqué issued by both terrorist cells gave him a *carte blanche* to speak for them.[14] However, it remained uncertain as to whether he was authorized to negotiate the substance of an agreement and settle for something less than the original terrorist demands, or simply make the arrangements for the release of the designated prisoners. Meanwhile, in Ottawa, Prime Minister Trudeau made it clear that the Government was not changing its position on the jailed terrorists when he stated that they "... are not political prisoners; they're bandits. That's why they're in jail." [15]

In analyzing the terrorist moves and the government responses during this period it is essential to attempt to separate the terrorist tactics of the FLQ cells and the military reactions which they provoked on the one hand, from the political strategy and long range aims of the FLQ and the political rationale behind the government's policies on the other. In such a dichotomy of tactics and strategy the kidnappings may be regarded as tactical moves in an overall strategy of what Gagnon and the

---

[11] Both statements nominated Robert Lemieux, a young Montreal lawyer who had defended several accused terrorists. *New York Times,* October 13, 1970.

[12] *Ibid.*

[13] Quoted in *The Milwaukee Journal,* October 12, 1970.

[14] *New York Times,* October 15, 1970.

[15] Quoted in *The Milwaukee Journal,* October 14, 1970.

FLQ called "political activity." Though it provoked a military response in the form of the War Measures Act on the tactical level, the Government nonetheless perceived its strategic intent when it articulated its own rationale for invoking the Act. Within this analytical structure, the necessity also arises to distinguish between the interests, power, and actions of the provincial government of Quebec and the interests, power, and policies of the federal Government in Ottawa. With this framework in mind the invocation of emergency powers assumes its rightful context.

The focus of action and attention at this point teetered between the diplonapping negotiations in Montreal and the government's decision and parliamentary debates in Ottawa. The first clue to the severity of the crisis and therefore to the possibility of using emergency powers might have been recognized in the appearance of the federal troops which were sent to Ottawa as early as October 13 in order to assist the Royal Canadian Mounted Police in guard duties. It was the first such use of troops in the capital in peacetime.[16] In Quebec, Premier Bourassa also requested federal troops in order to assure the security of the population. In answer to critics, Prime Minister Trudeau gave the rationale for this action which subsequently also served as the basis for the invocation of the War Measures Act itself:

I think the society must take every means at its disposal to defend itself against the emergence of a parallel power which defies the elected power in this country, and I think that goes to any distance.[17]

This specifically recognized the political nature of FLQ terrorism.

The War Measures Act was invoked on October 16, 1970, by Prime Minister Pierre Trudeau with a Proclamation which declared that Canada was threatened with insurrection by the activities of Le Front de Libération du Quebec.[18] The War Measures Act empowered the Government, without consulting Parliament, to enact its own laws concerning arrest, deportation, censorship and anything it might deem necessary for the security, defense, peace, order and welfare of Canada. Violations could be punished by five years' imprisonment and $5,000 fine with no trial, bail, or release without consent of the federal Minister of Justice. The Cabinet also adopted some supplementary Regulations which pro-

---

[16] Reported in *The Milwaukee Journal,* October 13, 1970.

[17] Quoted in the *New York Times,* October 16, 1970.

[18] The following account is based largely on the text of the Proclamation, excerpts from the Regulations and from Trudeau's statement, and news reports in the *New York Times,* October 17, 1970.

vided for emergency powers to deal with the insurrectionists. Stating that the FLQ advocated the use of force and the commission of crimes, including murder and kidnapping, as means of bringing about a governmental change in Canada, the Regulations declared the Front to be an unlawful association.

In his statement, Prime Minister Trudeau dwelt on the nature of the terrorist movement and his observations so echoed some of the conclusions in Chapter I that they bear repetition here:

... in recent years we have been forced to acknowledge the existence within Canada of a new and terrifying type of person—one who in earlier times would have been described as an anarchist but who is now known as a violent revolutionary. These persons allege that they are seeking social change through novel means. In fact, they are seeking the destruction of the social order through clandestine and violent means.

After discussing the Act itself, the Prime Minister again returned to the tactics and strategy of the revolutionaries:

... this extreme position into which governments have been forced is in some respects a trap. It is a well known technique of revolutionary groups who attempt to destroy society by unjustified violence to goad the authorities into inflexible attitudes. The revolutionaries then employ this evidence of alleged authoritarianism as justification for the need to use violence in their renewed attacks on the social structures.

I appeal to all Canadians not to become so obsessed by what the Government has done today in response to terrorism that they forget the opening play in this vicious game. That play was taken by the revolutionaries; they chose to use bombing, murder and kidnapping.

In an interview approximately six weeks later,[19] Prime Minister Trudeau reconfirmed his judgment that terrorism in Quebec had required "extraordinary measures" and that only the War Measures Act had been available to institute them. Arguing that a debate had been ruled out because " ... you can't arrest people quickly and break the back of an underground terrorist movement by giving them four or five days' notice," the Prime Minister maintained that the actual decision to invoke the Act had not been a difficult one, but that the question of timing was extremely important and had been discussed.

Following the invocation of the Act different reports estimated that from 150 to 300 arrests were made in over 150 raids. Among those arrested was Robert Lemieux, the negotiator for the two FLQ cells

[19] *The New York Times Magazine,* December 6, 1970.

involved in the kidnappings. In a news story, the *Montreal Gazette* stated that a confidential report of the Royal Canadian Mounted Police maintained that there were 22 active Front cells in Quebec with 130 members; it estimated that there were 2,000 inactive members, most of them young and many students.[20] Although some criticized the dragnet arrests, most Opposition criticism centered on the suspension of certain civil liberties in the Regulations adopted by the Cabinet.

Meanwhile, the negotiations between the FLQ kidnappers and the Quebec provincial government had resulted in a government offer to exchange five prisoners for the two kidnapped men. The government offer both for itself and for the federal Government. An October 16th country of their choice. A statement by the federal government's Foreign Minister made clear that the Quebec government was making the offer both for itself and for the federal Government. An October 16th government deadline (purposely set one hour before the War Measures Act was to be proclaimed) passed without an official FLQ answer, although Mr. Lemieux had rejected the offer as "incredible mockery." The provincial government regarded his reaction as a personal one and had continued to await a communiqué from the two FLQ cells. When the deadline passed without any response, however, Premier Bourassa appealed to the federal Government for armed forces to assist Montreal's police in guard duties. In Quebec, Trudeau again declined to meet the kidnappers' full demands for 23 prisoners, safe passage, and $500,000 in ransom. Giving in to such "blackmail," he said, would be to replace the legal system by the law of the jungle.[21]

On the following night, October 17, the body of Quebec Labor Minister Pierre Laporte was found in the trunk of a taxicab in downtown Montreal. The discovery of the body was made at approximately the same time Quebec Premier Bourassa delivered another plea to the kidnappers to return the two men safely in exchange for their own safe conduct to Cuba. Twelve hours later a letter in the handwriting of James Cross indicated that his kidnappers were still demanding the release of all 23 prisoners. Cross warned the authorities that his captors were serious and that it would be very dangerous for him if the police found their hideaway; he urged police to call off the search. (An intensified search for Cross and for Laporte's murderers had been undertaken throughout the city of Montreal. Quebec provincial police had issued

[20] Reported in the *New York Times,* October 17, 1970.
[21] Quoted in *The Milwaukee Journal,* October 17, 1970.

warrants for two Montreal men charged in both kidnappings; a third man had been sought since the Cross kidnapping.)

At the governmental level Prime Minister Trudeau held a two-hour meeting with his Cabinet and then flew to Montreal where he conferred with the Mayor of Montreal and Quebec's Premier. But his previous refusal to release the 23 prisoners was not modified. Instead, the Government repeated its offer of free passage to Cuba for the kidnappers if they freed Cross unharmed. With regard to the Laporte murder, Prime Minister Trudeau denounced the assassination as a "cruel and senseless" act and stated:

> ... The men responsible for these crimes are not representative Canadians. They are members of a hard core devoted to a single purpose—to inspire within all of us fear and hatred, and in this atmosphere to destroy our nation .... Those responsible for this crime will be found and will be dealt with in the calm and dispassionate atmosphere of Canadian courts. The F.L.Q. has sown the seeds of its own destruction. It has revealed that it has no mandate but terror, no policies but violence and no solutions but murder.[22]

Canadian leaders throughout the country expressed similar feelings of shock, sorrow, and shame. In a show of support for a hard-line suppression of terrorism, the Canadian House of Commons voted on October 19 with a majority of 190 to 16 to endorse the government's proclamation of emergency powers under the War Measures Act. As of the end of October, 1970, there was no new word on the fate of James Cross, nor any public indication that the diplonappers would accept the government's counter-offer of safe passage to Cuba (the last published communication from either Cross or his abductors was that of October 18th).

Before continuing with developments in the Cross diplonapping, a brief outline of the follow-up to the Laporte assassination might be appropriate here. On November 6, 1970, a 19-year-old student, Bernard Lortie, was arrested in Montreal as a key suspect in the case. Lortie admitted his participation in the kidnapping of Laporte, but denied any involvement in his murder. He identified his accomplices as Paul Rose, Jacques Rose, and Francis Simard. Lortie stated that Laporte had been kidnapped because it seemed to the terrorists that the abduction of James Cross was not "proving effective." [23] (As had been indicated, the Laporte kidnapping took place only fifteen minutes after the Quebec

---

[22] *The New York Times Magazine,* December 6, 1970.
[23] Reported in the *New York Times,* November 8, 1970.

provincial government had rejected the Front's demand for the release of 23 FLQ prisoners.) The three other suspects identified by Lortie were arrested in a raid on a farm house south of Montreal on December 28th. One of them, Paul Rose, had also been sought in connection with the Cross kidnapping. Murder charges were filed against all four kidnappers in early January, 1971, and in mid-March Rose was found guilty of the murder of Laporte and was sentenced to life imprisonment. Francis Simard also received a life sentence for participation in the murder and in September, 1971, Bernard Lortie was convicted of the kidnapping of Laporte and was subsequently sentenced to twenty years' imprisonment.[24] The trial of Jacques Rose on the kidnapping charge began in March, 1972, and its results were unknown as of the date of this writing.

The accusations and counter-accusations which ensued during the latter part of October and throughout the rest of the year between the government and opposition parties as well as between Ottawa and Quebec separatists, though of interest, are less relevant here than the continued negotiations between government representatives and the FLQ which ultimately culminated in the release of James Cross. Suffice it to say that Prime Minister Trudeau constantly emphasized what he described as the "full agreement" between all governments concerned in the policies adopted toward the kidnappers and in the measures taken for Canadian internal security. In response to those accusing Ottawa of trying to impose its will on Quebec, Trudeau stated: "All that each Government did was to exercise its own powers in the sole interest of collective security." [25]

In the light of a terrorist strategy partially aimed at fomenting conditions conducive to revolution, it should be noted that there were those who believed that the division between Quebec and the rest of Canada had been deepened and that the cause of Quebec separatism had been strengthened by the crisis created by the FLQ kidnappings. Although numerous Quebec leaders had denounced the kidnappings themselves and were outraged by the assassination of Pierre Laporte, there appeared to be growing resentment over the severity of the actions taken under the War Measures Act. Official figures on those actions were given by Quebec's Minister of Justice in response to written questions submitted to him by the House leader of Parti Quebecois in early December.[26]

[24] Reported in *The Milwaukee Journal,* March 14 and September 23, 1971.

[25] Reported and quoted in *The Globe and Mail* (Toronto), November 2, 1970.

[26] Reported in *ibid.,* December 3, 1970.

From October 16, 1970, when the Act was proclaimed, to November 24, 1970, police carried out 3,068 raids and arrested 453 persons. Among those charged as a result of the raids, students were most numerous; though the ages of those arrested varied from 14 to 58, 252 were between the ages of 19 and 25. Materials seized included 159 fire-arms, 677 sticks of dynamite, 912 detonators, and 4,962 rounds of ammunition.

The invocation of the Act itself, however, had been defended not only by Prime Minister Trudeau, but also by the Premier of Quebec, Robert Bourassa.[27] Admitting that the Act presented "the most delicate and difficult decision" he had faced, Bourassa continued : "The lesson I have learned is that you cannot give in to blackmail or there will be no end. If we would have given in on the prisoners, it would have been an invitation for other terrorists or would-be-terrorist activities." Emphasizing that the most important element in withdrawing troops would be whether the kidnappers and the killers of Laporte were found, the Premier stated his own belief that the results of both police action and court cases would determine whether the terrorist movement had been caught at its roots. As Trudeau had done earlier, Premier Bourassa's statement indicated his understanding of the nature of the problem of diplomatic kidnappings when he said, "We are facing a new kind of terror—political kidnapping in North America."

In attempting to control the terrorists and at the same time appease the critics of the Regulations adopted under the War Measures Act, the Government proposed an anti-terrorist bill to replace the Regulations. Like them, it outlawed the FLQ and related terrorist groups and extended, though in modified form, the extraordinary police powers granted in the Regulations under the Act. The thirteen-day House debate on the new bill was particularly bitter and in terms of parliamentary time one of the most costly proposals sponsored by the Trudeau Government since it had assumed power over two years before. In debate, opposition members argued that anti-terrorist measures would not solve the real problems in Quebec and that if there had been a need for emergency powers to deal with terrorism it had passed. One back-bencher stated that the situation had become "totally different" and that "underlying it is the need for social and economic improvement." [28] All three oppo-

---

[27] The following is based on a report of Premier Bourassa's speech in the *New York Times,* November 15, 1970.

[28] Quoted in *The Globe and Mail* (Toronto), November 27, 1970.

sition parties criticized the bill although it was ultimately adopted by Parliament as a Public Order Act in early December, 1970.

Meanwhile, speculation continued regarding the fate of James Cross. In early November Canadian authorities stated that they had been sent a photograph of Cross from the FLQ as evidence of his still being alive, but no word was received from Cross himself until November 22nd when two French-language newspapers published a letter from him dated November 15th. [29] The letter stated that he was in good health and was being well treated. In part it compared his situation with that of the FLQ prisoners: "I have heard about the treatment of the F.L.Q. political prisoners in jail and I am quite sure that I am better treated than them... They consider me a political prisoner and they will keep me in captivity as long as the authorities do not accept their demands." A personal letter was also sent to his wife.

Later, after Cross had been freed, he severely criticized the press for its speculation about the letters he had written while held as hostage and indicated that it had resulted in "four rough days" for him and could have cost him his life.[30] He was particularly angered that the press had accepted the letters as expressions of his own thoughts and stated that all of the letters, except those to his wife, had been dictated to him. This obviously accounted for his references (above) to the FLQ "political prisoners" and their treatment. In addition, Cross stated that by misspelling several words in his letters he had tried to indicate that he was writing under duress; however, he equally objected to press speculation that that was what he was trying to do. Such reports, he said, built up a sense of hostility between him and his kidnappers who thought he was trying to trick them.

At the same time that the Cross letter of November 15th was published, the FLQ released a communiqué to the people of Quebec on behalf of the "Liberation Cell" which had kidnapped Cross.[31] The communiqué 1) accused the police of resorting to torture in order to uncover the Cross hideout, 2) urged U.N. Secretary-General U Thant to publicly endorse the "liberation struggles" of the Quebec people, denounce the use of torture, and act as an intermediary between the

[29] Published in *Quebec-Presse* and *Journal de Montreal* and reported in *The Globe and Mail* (Toronto), November 23, 1970.

[30] Reported in *The Milwaukee Journal,* December 10, 1970. See also the Cross interview in *The Globe and Mail* (Toronto), December 10, 1970.

[31] Reported in *The Globe and Mail* (Toronto), November 23, 1970.

Canadian Government and the FLQ, and 3) told the newspapers to stop spreading false rumors about the FLQ and instead publish the truth about slums, unemployment, and corruption. In an interview, an FLQ leader stated bluntly that Cross would die if police found out where he was being held.

Fortunately, events transpired differently. On December 4, 1970, Cuban intermediaries released James Cross to Canadian authorities at the site of the Expo '67 world fair after the Canadian Government had flown his kidnappers to political asylum in Cuba. The ransom negotiations took place after police had located the hideout house in North Montreal on December 2nd and had surrounded it. Responding to the kidnappers' offer to negotiate, a government representative, Robert Demers, and Bernard Mergler, an attorney who had defended FLQ members previously, both entered the kidnappers' building and worked out the details. They arranged for Cross and his abductors to drive under police escort to the Canadian pavilion at the Expo site which had been declared temporary Cuban territory; there they met the acting Cuban Consul who detained Cross until after word was received that the seven persons who were provided with safe conduct to Cuba had arrived in Havana.[32] Although the federal Minister of Justice first stated that all seven would be "exiles for life," he later admitted that only the actual kidnappers would be prosecuted if they returned.

Cross himself was released in good physical and mental condition. His obvious relief at being rescued unharmed was expressed in the following words: "I am very happy to come back to the world. There were times in the past eight weeks when I had almost given up hope."[33] He indicated that his worst moment came when he heard on the radio that Labor Minister Pierre Laporte had been killed by another cell of the FLQ. Although Cross's own kidnappers had been uninformed about Laporte's kidnapping in advance, Cross indicated that his own impression was that they had known about Laporte's murder before the official announcement. When questioned as to what official policies should be toward the diplonappings, Cross stated that he could not

[32] "The seven persons on the Havana flight were Carbonneau; Lanctot and his wife and child; Jacques Cosette Trudel, Lanctot's brother-in-law, and his wife; and Pierre Seguin, not otherwise identified." Reported in *The Milwaukee Journal*, December 4, 1970. (It was subsequently reported that Seguin was one of the kidnappers.)

[33] Quoted in *ibid.*

decide what a government should do in the event of a political kidnapping —stand its ground or capitulate.[34] Nonetheless, in the same interview following his release Cross not only thanked the Governments of Canada and of Quebec for arranging the negotiations which made it possible for his release, but also thanked the Government of Cuba for having accepted the kidnappers.

Of particular interest for the purposes of this analysis are the views of the terrorists themselves, their own rationale for the kidnapping, and their assessment of its success or failure. Cross himself regarded his kidnappers as "fervent and convinced revolutionaries" who had set their aims and objectives as "establishing a revolutionary state in Quebec by means of violence." [35] Additional insights may be gleaned from a ninety-minute tape recording of discussions between four of the cell members responsible for the Cross kidnapping which was published in the Toronto newspaper, *The Globe and Mail*.[36] From the tape it appears evident that although only four cell members took part in the actual kidnapping, others participated in the planning and were still at large in Montreal. The kidnappers said that they only decided the night before the kidnapping that they would kidnap Cross rather than the U.S. consul in Montreal. They chose Cross, according to the tape, because they thought that the abduction of a British official would make a greater impact on Quebec's English-speaking community.

In their assessment of the success of the kidnapping itself, the terrorists were in agreement that it had failed in all but one of its aims. They were successful, they felt, in forcing the publication and broadcast of the FLQ communiqué. They admitted, however, that they were equally concerned with securing the release of the FLQ "political prisoners" in which objective, of course, they had failed. During their discussion, the kidnappers also referred to the fact that the two kidnappings had shown a new kind of cooperation which took place between the different cells

[34] He indicated that "the best possible answer was the one that was achieved, namely the police surrounding the house and therefore the kidnappers letting me go alive, go free, alive in return for their own lives. I can see no other guarantee that you can reach. If you let these chaps go to Cuba, what guarantee is there that I would then be released? You see, this is the interminable dilemma, and I'm too close to the situation now to give any reasoned judgment. I simply don't know. I'm sorry." Interview printed in *The Globe and Mail* (Toronto), December 10, 1970.
[35] *Ibid.*
[36] The following account was reported in *The Globe aid Mail* (Toronto), December 5, 1970.

of the FLQ—the Liberation Cell, the Chenier Cell (held responsible for the Laporte kidnapping), and the Viger communications cell. One member stated: "These cells are in communication with each other by fairly cautious and fairly personal methods but I think that this phenomenon, communication between cells of the Front, is completely new."

Finally, the tape made it clear that the terrorists were surprised by what they regarded as Prime Minister Trudeau's "unwillingness" to negotiate. They expected, they said, that within a week after the kidnapping at the most the Government would agree to negotiate. One speaker attributed the Prime Minister's refusal to negotiate partly to his "stubborn" character and partly to pressures from Washington; he suggested that a policy of negotiating would set a bad precedent for U.S. Government dealings with groups such as the Black Panthers and the Weatherman faction of the SDS if they were to use the same tactics sometime in the future. With news in early 1971 of the planned kidnapping of Special Assistant to the President, Henry Kissinger, this suggestion that the kidnapping tactic might be seized upon by radicals in the United States and be adopted to their own purposes becames less of an abstract idea and more of a concrete danger.

Several notes and tapes from the FLQ were subsequently found and published. One communiqué,[37] dated December 5, 1970, stressed the point that the FLQ was not dead. Jointly signed by a number of cells in Quebec, the communiqué stated that the Cross kidnapping was in fact a "victory" for the FLQ because it required 22,000 men and 60 days to find the kidnappers. A second tape,[38] with the voices of the same four cell members recorded on the first one, stated that in order to maintain a revolutionary climate, the FLQ would have to resort in the future to illegal actions which would be more and more spectacular. Specifically mentioned was the need to plan bombings in places where the targets would have more political significance than in the past. Pointing out that indiscriminate bombing waves in the past had spread fear among ordinary French-speaking residents—the very people the FLQ claimed to be liberating—one speaker maintained, "If we limit ourselves to Anglophone districts, we can create the desired effect in a rather controlled state, which means there will not be any spill-overs into the Francophone side."

[37] Reported in *ibid.*, December 7, 1970.
[38] *Ibid.*

Throughout 1971 conditions remained too unsettled to speculate whether these threats would be carried out or whether, in fact, the anti-terrorist legislation and police arrests based on it had to any degree struck at the roots of the FLQ movement. In January, the Canadian Government ended its deployment of armed forces in Quebec, Montreal, and Ottawa where they had been sent to assist police in anti-terrorist activities.[39] This decision, involving the withdrawal of 5,000 troops, was reached after a request from the Quebec Minister of Justice. However, the Public Order Act, the anti-terrorist legislation which replaced the Regulations under the War Measures Act, remained in force and Prime Minister Trudeau stated that it was still too early to withdraw it. The Canadian body politic at best was divided and the Quebec separatists continued to promote their political and economic program for an independent Quebec.

In setting the Canadian diplonapping cases in the perspective of urban guerilla terrorism, certain salient features emerge in relation both to the revolutionary strategy of the terrorists themselves and to the policy implications to be derived from the specific case outcomes. Chapter I has emphasized that the political kidnappings figure as only one type of terrorist tactic in a political strategy aimed at eventual governmental overthrow or, in the interim, at fomenting an atmosphere of public chaos and governmental atrophy. Their intermediate aims may include monetary ransom, release of so-called political prisoners and/or political asylum for the kidnappers themselves, but the instigation of terror within the populace at large and within the governmental elites remains basic to their purposes. If the government over-reacts with a policy of suppression, this in turn can be manipulated to the advantage of the terrorists by drawing to their cause the sympathies of the otherwise apolitical masses.

With this strategy in mind, the Cross and Laporte kidnappings taken together were less than totally successful. The Cross kidnapping produced neither the monetary ransom of $500,000 nor the release of the 23 FLQ prisoners; it did, however, secure refuge for the kidnappers and their families with political asylum in Cuba. Moreover, it was when both the Quebec provincial government and the federal Government rejected the dual ransom demands in exchange for Cross's freedom, that a second cell of the FLQ kidnapped Laporte and thus escalated the level of terrorist pressure. Taking the Laporte kidnapping in con-

---

[39] ·Reported in the *New York Times,* January 6, 1971.

junction with that of Cross, a slightly different picture emerges. Although, once again, the demands for ransom and release of prisoners were rejected, the Government reacted strongly to the Laporte kidnapping with the invocation of the War Measures Act just dix days later. The following day, almost as if in response, Laporte was found murdered.

A pattern of escalation and counter-escalation as between the Government and the involved FLQ cells was thus instituted. This, in turn, contributed to increased political criticism by their mutual critics of what were considered to be extreme measures taken on both sides. In other words, although non-radical separatists strongly condemned the FLQ murder of Pierre Laporte, they became almost equally critical of the police arrests and other anti-terrorist measures pursued by the Government under the War Measures Act. In parallel terms, pro-Government supporters who where critical of the separatist movement to begin with—even in its nonviolent constitutional form—became increasingly distrustful of all separatists, not only the FLQ terrorists. Thus, the already present divisions between government and opposition parties and between Quebec and the rest of Canada were deepened even more by the two kidnappings and by the governmental policies dealing with them.

Because of the different reactions of the two cells to the provincial government's negotiating offers, any generalization about the wisdom of the policies pursued can be only tentative. Within the revolutionary matrix of FLQ terrorism, a policy of "minimizing the rewards" by refusing to accede to the kidnappers' ransom demands was partially followed but achieved only marginal success. Neither the demand for ransom money nor that for the release of all 23 prisoners was met. Although the government compromised somewhat and offered the release of five prisoners and safe conduct for them and the kidnappers to a country of their choice in exchange for both Cross and Laporte, this was rejected and Pierre Laporte was murdered. In the case of Cross, however, safe conduct to asylum in Cuba for the kidnappers and their families was ultimately agreed upon and Cross was set free. The very fact that asylum was available, of course, prevents the complete institution of a policy of "no rewards." The variables in the two cases also affected their outcome and included: 1) the kidnappings were carried out by two different cells with perhaps different aims or priorities, 2) the imposition of the War Measures Act had increased the powers and numbers of the police considerably, and 3) the Laporte hideout had not been discovered by the police prior to his death, whereas that of Cross had been uncovered.

In conclusion, then, it was in fact the increased security measures and their attendant risks which were more effective in deterring the Cross kidnappers from murder and in securing his release than the policy of minimal rewards. Minimizing the rewards, as Chapter VIII will discuss in greater detail, is largely a policy of deterrence and can only be judged in the context of how it affects or prevents future potential kidnappings; it is obviously less persuasive in influencing the kidnappers' actions once a kidnapping has occurred and must then be coupled with a policy of increasing the riks to them of any subsequent actions of intransigence or extreme violence. Most important, the Canadian cases clearly illustrate the advantages of maintaining a certain amount of flexibility and a constant willingness to communicate over what is negotiable, if not to negotiate the specific demands themselves.

CHAPTER VIII

CONCLUSIONS AND SOME POLICY RECOMMENDATIONS

The diplonappings—and how to deal with them—have raised several practical problems with both legal parameters and political repercussions. In order to examine the diplomatic kidnappings in a legal perspective, Chapters II, III, and IV have analyzed the relevant customs and principles of international law as well as the international conventions and treaties which apply to them. Thus, Chapter II attempted to define the nature of diplomatic inviolability and to identify some of its major legal per-quisites; Chapter III examined state responsibility and the obligations of host governments for the protection and security of aliens in general and of diplomats in particular; and Chapter IV reviewed the legal status of political asylum, especially as it has evolved in Latin America, and the extent and limitations of extradition. Chapter I set the phenomenon of diplomatic kidnapping within the context of urban terrorism, while Chapters V, VI, and VII dealt with actual case studies of recent diplo-nappings and some of the policy problems created by them for the diplomats and governments concerned. It remains therefore for this section, Chapter VIII, to draw together the legal precepts and the political realities in an attempt to elicit from them some positive policy recom-mendations for future governmental action.

Although the analysis of such policies can perhaps best be developed by breaking down the problem into some of its component parts, it must be emphasized at the outset that the key to these policy recommendations is the concept of prevention. As simple as this sounds, it carries with it some basic but implicit assumptions which are not entirely self-evident on the surface. It assumes, first of all, that deterrence is possible; that if adequate security and other preventive policies are adopted, the diplo-nappers can, in fact, be deterred. This in turn assumes that the kidnappers are rational, can draw the proper conclusions from previous governmental statements and actions, and will weigh the actual risks involved against the potential rewards in any actions they undertake. Secondly, the concept of prevention assumes that the problem of diplonapping has escalated to a level where it can no longer be tolerated as a mere fact of international life and that the governments most concerned must and can act jointly to institute preventive measures. Finally, prevention implies the adoption of policies which will both "maximize the risks" and "minimize the rewards" which can reasonably be expected by those contemplating a diplonapping attempt. This means both increased security measures in order to make any kidnapping attempt as difficult and dangerous as possible, and a firm position on no ransom and no asylum if such security measures do not immediately succeed. The latter policy of minimizing the rewards by refusing to accede to ransom demands is, of course, the most difficult to deal with—both politically and morally.

In reviewing some of the legal concepts involved, it has been pointed out repeatedly that diplomatic inviolability has become a well-established principle in international law both through international custom and general practice and in international treaties and conventions. Wilson, for example, maintains that:

The fundamental and universally accepted principles of personal inviolability and immunity from civil and criminal jurisdiction were restated and reinforced through practice, municipal legislation, judicial decisions, and declarations by writers, jurists, and statesmen.[1]

The Vienna Convention on Diplomatic Relations of 1961 has been cited as a widely recognized and accepted guide to the current law and practice of diplomatic privileges and immunities. In it, Article 29 clearly provides for the personal inviolability of diplomatic officers. Article 41 of the Vienna Convention on Consular Relations contains a similar provision for consular inviolability. Although states disagree to some extent on the rules concerning lower diplomatic personnel, liberalizing trends toward more extensive immunities have emerged. Since 1945, for example, the treaties and agreements regulating American economic assistance missions overseas have usually provided for full diplomatic immunity for the members of such missions. In general, members of military missions, information personnel, various attachés, and some technical and administrative personnel have been similarly designated as possessing diplomatic status.[2]

---

[1] Wilson, Clifton E., *Diplomatic Privileges and Immunities, op. cit.,* p. 273.
[2] *Ibid.,* p. 275.

Such status is important for this analysis of the diplomatic kidnappings in that the special "protection" owed to foreign diplomats by host governments arises from the principle of their personal inviolability *as diplomats*. That obligation of protection, as discussed in Chapter III, has been as firmly established in international law as the diplomatic inviolability upon which it is based. A summary of the changing nature of diplomatic privileges and immunities thus concludes:

The diplomat continued to enjoy *the right of protection* which was usually provided in both normal circumstances and when diplomats were threatened with death or injury. In addition, primarily through their legal codes, most nations provided satisfactory punishment of individuals for offenses committed against diplomats.[3]

This "right of protection," however, is accorded only to those with diplomatic status. It is quite clear from the press accounts of the case studies examined in Chapters V, VI, and VII and from the statements of the governments concerned, that the vast majority of those agents kidnapped were in fact regarded as possessing diplomatic status.

In the abortive diplonapping attempts discussed under Category One, there was no question about the diplomatic status either of Curtis C. Cutter, U.S. Consul in Porto Alegre, Brazil, or of John Gordan Mein, U.S. Ambassador to Guatemala, who was assassinated in a 1968 ambush and kidnapping attempt. Following the Mein assassination, the United States Government demanded a full investigation from the Guatemalan Government which immediately proclaimed a state of martial law and subsequently offered a substantial reward for any information leading to the arrest of the assailants. In the three most highly publicized diplonappings of Category Two, the Elbrick, von Holleben, and Bucher cases, all three diplomats were ambassadors and clearly possessed the diplomatic inviolability which entitled them to special governmental protection. As the host government, the Brazilian Government acceded to the kidnappers' demands in all three cases and released fifteen, forty, and seventy prisoners respectively. Moreover, in the Elbrick case, the Brazilian Government subsequently carried on intensive investigations which resulted in a Government report that eighteen persons had been involved in the kidnapping and four had been arrested; others were supposedly in hiding in Cuba.

Four of the other case studies in Category Two involved foreign governmental personnel of less than ambassadorial rank, but clearly

---

[3] *Ibid.*, p. 274. (Italics added.)

possessing diplomatic status. An Air Attaché at the U.S. Embassy in Santo Domingo, the Dominican Republic, was released in exchange for twenty political prisoners; a poliitcal secretary in the U.S. Embassy in Guatemala was exchanged for three political prisoners; and five political prisoners were released in exchange for the freedom of the Japanese Consul-General in São Paulo, Brazil. In all three cases the political prisoners sought and received political asylum in Mexico.[4] In the fourth case, involving the son of a Swiss Consul in Colombia and the first secretary of the Swiss Embassy, ransom money was demanded for their freedom and was ultimately paid. In all four cases the host governments obviously believed that they did have an obligation of special protection toward diplomatic personnel which, when violated, obligated them to take special measures for the release of the diplomats concerned. The case of Brazilian Consul Diás Gomide in Uruguay and that of the Honorary Consul of Britain, Stanley Sylvester, in Argentina are less illustrative of Category Two cases since, although ransom demands were met, the money and food respectively were provided by nongovernmental sources. In neither case, however, was the obligation of governmental protection denied, and both governments pursued the kidnappers in thorough and extensive searches. Because of the lack of adequate information, it is difficult to place the Draper case in either Category Two or Three; regardless of this, it was clear that his diplomatic status was never at issue.

The diplonapping cases in Categories Three and Four (those involving a refusal of the host governments to accede to the demands of the kidnappers) are more ambiguous in terms of their import for the concepts of diplomatic inviolability and state responsibility for special protection. In the diplonapping of the Paraguayan consul in Argentina, for example, there simply was not enough information published to develop an informed and objective assessment of the actual legal position of the Argentine Government. In two communiqués to the Argentine Embassy in Washington, D.C., the Government maintained that one of the designated "prisoners" was in fact a fugitive from justice still at large and that the other was already being prosecuted for nonpolitical crimes by a federal court; his case, therefore, was no longer under the jurisdiction of the executive branch. The diplomatic status of the Paraguayan consul was apparently not in question, however, for the second com-

---

[4] The problems involving the granting or refusal of political asylum are discussed below, pp. 138-141.

muniqué specifically referred to him as a "diplomatic officer." As was reported in Chapter V, the consul was freed despite Argentina's refusal to accede to the kidnappers' demands.

The Spanish kidnapping of the Honorary West German Consul, Eugen Beihl, was also complicated in its implications for the principle of state responsibility for special protection both because Beihl was an *Honorary* consul and because the circumstances surrounding his release were so unique. Thus, his kidnappers had not demanded the freedom of any political prisoners in exchange for Beihl's release, but rather asked for lenient treatment of the Basque prisoners awaiting court-martial sentences in Burgos. Moreover, because the E.T.A. released Consul Beihl before the verdict was pronounced and before President Franco's commutation of the six death sentences, it was difficult to ascertain the precise effect of their action. It could not be concluded definitely that the commutation was made because of a secret bargain with the E.T.A., because of the dangers of greater internal turmoil, or in response to international pressures.

The kidnapping and ultimate murder of West German Ambassador Karl von Spreti provide a much clearer illustration of governmental attitudes and policies toward the international legal principles of diplomatic inviolability and state responsibility for special protection of diplomatic personnel. Although the Government of Guatemala originally stated that it would do "everything in its power" to obtain the Ambassador's safe return, it was soon made abundantly clear that this did not include the release of the seventeen (ultimately twenty-two) political prisoners demanded by the Rebel Armed Forces. The Guatemalan Government's legal position was based on the argument that since the political prisoners had already been tried and convicted, they could not be freed by executive orders; Guatemalan law prohibited the granting of amnesty for any convicted prisoners without approval of the national judiciary. Therefore, the Government stated, it was impossible legally to accede to the kidnappers' demands. Though Guatemala thereby emphasized the legal aspects of the case, its argument was grounded in Guatemalan domestic law, not in international law.

It was international law, however, to which the Government of the Federal Republic of Germany appealed in its denunciation of the Guatemalan position. Stating that it was "disappointed" with Guatemalan inaction, the West German Government went even further and maintained that it "could not accept" the decision of the Government of Guatemala not to exchange the prisoners for Ambassador von Spreti. As mentioned in Chapter VI, the Federal Republic was supported in its position by several ambassadors in Guatemala who also protested the Government's decision. This criticism of Guatemala's actions in the von Spreti case was basesd firmly on international law, its provisions for diplomatic inviolability, and its requirements of protection for diplomatic agents. The West German Government made quite clear its view that Guatemala was derelict not only in its failure te secure the Ambassador's release, but also in failing to provide adequate protection for him in the first place. In reducing the Federal Republic's diplomatic relations with Guatemala to a bare minimum, West German Foreign Minister Walter Scheel stated publicly that because Guatemala had not been able to provide the protection "required by international law," the Federal Republic had decided that it had to recall its chief of mission.

It might be appropriate at this point to review exactly what the requirements of "special protection" entail. Chapter III dealt in some detail with the question of state responsibility and pointed out that under international law states are obligated to exercise due diligence to prevent acts by private persons on their territory injurious to other states— such as attacks upon the personal inviolability of diplomats. If prevention is not possible, then punishment and/or reparations are required. States are thus obligated to provide both protection and reparations when private violations of international law result in injury to aliens. The degree of the protection required, however, is highly ambiguous and usually defined as the exercise of "due diligence" according to the circumstances of any particular case. For example, in cases involving recurrent or notorious dangers or where special conditions exist, a greater degree of protection is expected. In addition, of course, all diplomats require special protection regardless of the circumstances—a protection which arises out of their personal inviolability. The responsibility to provide protection obliges the host government both to *prevent* violations of their person and, if prevention is impossible, to *punish* severely the violators.

It is evident from the circumstances in which the von Spreti diplonapping occured that Guatemala was in a state of political turmoil, that terrorism was both notorious and recurrent, and that a series of previous kidnappings provided some evidence of "special conditions" requiring greater than normal vigilance. In applying the requirements of special protection and due diligence to the von Spreti diplonapping, therefore, one could interpret the position of the Federal Republic of Germany as in effect arguing that neither the special protection required by the status of the Ambassador nor the exercise of due diligence required by extraordinary circumstances were provided. Obviously, if provided, they had not been sufficient to prevent the kidnapping. Without direct knowledge of all of the security provisions afforded by the Guatemalan Government, however, it would be both difficult and presumptuous to conclude definitely that Guatemala was legally derelict by not *attempting* to prevent the incident. According to Eagleton, due diligence has been exercised if the government concerned did not omit anything practical or possible which ought to have been done and if it employed all of the means within its reach.[5] Despite past U.S. arguments that the diligence required must be commensurate with the emergency or with the results of negligence, most authorities agree that the disastrous results of preventive attempts which have failed do not of themselves create state negligence.

Of primary concern for the purpose of this analysis is not the determination of Guatemala's legal responsibility, but the degree to which international norms of state responsibility were actually applied to the case and recognized by the states involved. In this regard, the Government of Guatemala did not refer to international law either to refute the West German charges or to bolster its own defense. Rather, it based its arguments upon Guatemalan domestic law and responded as much to the pressures of political expediency as to the law itself. The Government of the Federal Republic of Germany, in contrast, though basically concerned about the release of its Ambassador, protested against the Guatemalan Government's actions not only because of its refusal to free the political prisoners, but also because of its initial failure to prevent the diplonapping and so protect the Ambassador's life. The Federal Republic also evidenced its concern for the international implications of the diplomatic kidnapping by calling on friendly governments for "international measures" to improve the protection of diplomats in the future.

Before examining what some of those measures might be, the Mitrione kidnapping in Uruguay may provide some additional insights into the applicability to the recent diplonapping cases of the concepts of diplomatic inviolability and state responsibility for protection. Although Mitrione, as a United States A.I.D. advisor to the Uruguayan police force, was hardly a "traditional" diplomat, his diplomatic status was never raised as an issue, either legally or politically. Since most American A.I.D. personnel have been accorded diplomatic immunity by treaty and have been considered as *bona fide* members of U.S. missions overseas,

[5] See Chapter III, pp. 46-47.

it is not surprising that the question did not arise. Had the United States taken a somewhat different and more critical stance toward Uruguay, however, the diplomatic status of Mitrione could have been a key factor in any legal assessment of the case. Since "special protection" can only be demanded for diplomats or in special conditions, any assertion that Uruguay was negligent in not providing special protection would depend for its validity on the legal requirement of such protection in the first place. The United States abrogated the need for any further examination of Mitrione's status when it did not in any way hold Uruguay responsible for failing to prevent his kidnapping and assassination.

As related in Chapter VI, the Government of Uruguay refused to negotiate with the Tupamaro kidnappers because it did not recognize the Tupamaros as a legitimate political group or party. The Government also attempted to distinguish between Tupamaro prisoners and other prisoners on the same basis; it argued that "political prisoners" did not include the Tupamaros whom it regarded as "common criminals." Despite some initial rumors to the contrary, the President of Uruguay remained adamant in his refusal to negotiate with the Tupamaros and labelled their demands as attempted extortion against the Government. In an official statement explaining its position after Mitrione's murder, the Government maintained it was not "legally possible, honorable or conducive to anything" for the Government to negotiate with criminal organizations, even to save innocent lives. The reason why it was not "legally possible" to negotiate was not elaborated upon and remains questionable; the argument that it would not be "conducive to anything," however, requires some further examination.

As seen above, Brazil (having acceded to similar demands of diplo-nappers at home) was openly critical in its indignation and protest over the Uruguayan refusal to release prisoners in ransom for the Brazilian Consul kidnapped at the same time as Mitrione. In contrast, the United States followed a markedly different policy toward Uruguay in the Mitrione case. Although the United States Ambassador to Uruguay denounced the assassination as a crime against humanity and the U.S. Government in Washington condemned the inhumanity of the terrorists, neither was directly critical of the Government of Uruguay for its refusal to release the political prisoners in trade for Mitrione. In its first state-ment of policy regarding the diplonappings in general, the United States Department of State reiterated that the U.S. Government had urged the Uruguayan Government to do "everything possible" to secure Mitrione's release; however, it had not pressured Uruguay "literally" to accede to the kidnappers' demands. The State Department maintained that such accession would encourage other terrorists to attempt to kidnap more Americans in the future. If extremists believed that their demands would be supported by the United States if they kidnapped and held Americans as prisoners, the State Department spokesman argued, it might mean "great risks for all Americans overseas." [6] This argument is presumably what the Uruguayan Government had in mind when it maintained that negotiations with the terrorists would not be conducive to anything.

Any consideration of policy alternatives, such as that of refusing to accede to any diplonapping demands regardless of the consequences, immediately raises the key concept of prevention. Will future diplomatic kidnappings be prevented by "minimizing the rewards"? In this survey of recent diplomatic kidnappings in Latin America, Canada, and elsewhere, the evidence has not all been published, and what is available is inconclusive. For example, if one attempts to relate the diplonapping and murder of Ambassador von Spreti in Guatemala in early April, 1970, to the diplonapping and release of the Paraguayan Consul, Waldemar Sanchez, in Argentina in late March, 1970, several enigmatic queries spring to mind. One is whether the Guatemalan kidnappers of von Spreti were aware of the Argentine case and of the refusal of the Argentine Government to release any prisoners as ransom; if so, they were not deterred by that example of a policy of "no rewards." Even when there were no rewards in their own case, they did not follow the more humanitarian example of their Argentine counterparts, but retaliated with the murder of von Spreti. Another query is whether the no reward stance of the Argentine Government and the lack of reprisal on the part of the Argentine kidnappers figured in the decision of the Guatemalan Government to be equally adamant in their refusal to accede to the demands of the Guatemalan diplonappers. One may ask similar questions with regard to subsequent cases in Uruguay, Brazil, Canada, and Turkey: why were the prospective kidnappers not deterred by the precedents of no reward in both Argentina and Guatemala? Here again, the policy of prevention by deterrence through minimizing the rewards did not succeed in practice.

Before abandoning such a policy as being without merit, however, there are other factors to be considered. Of greatest importance are the numerous cases in which the governments involved ultimately acceded to the demands of the diplonappers and thus provided the rewards

[6] Quoted in the *New York Times,* August 11, 1970.

sought and successful precedents for future attempts. Even a cursory examination of the four categories of diplonappings will immediately indicate that Category Two (those cases in which the diplonappers' demands—whether for political prisoners, for publicity, or for ransom money—were met) leads all the others in the number of cases recorded. At least nine [7] such diplonappings have taken place since 1969, two more which are questionable as to category (Draper and Beihl), and several non-diplomatic kidnappings in which demands made were fully met. In contrast, Categories Three and Four together (cases of governmental refusals to meet diplonapper demands) include only four definite cases of no rewards whatsoever [8]—and three questionable (Draper, Beihl, and Jackson)—all of them having occurred since late March, 1970. Although no prisoners were released in exchange for James Cross, his kidnappers themselves were granted asylum in a bargaining exchange.

It is not too illogical to surmise, therefore, that the previous precedents of "maximized rewards," being both more numerous and having taken place over a longer period of time, have had a greater impact on the diplonappers' expectations than the very few and very recent precedents of "minimized rewards." Obviously, if such is the case, the few failures of the no ransom policy in no way detract from the intrinsic merit and possible future success of a policy of minimizing rewards which, if followed consistently, will in turn become the established precedent, rather than the exception to it. In addition, it should be pointed out that the suggestion of developing concerted policies, and therefore a consistent precedent of "minimized rewards," is almost always coupled with the parallel suggestion of "maximizing the risks" involved. Such a policy should not be discarded, therefore, as an isolated technique which in and of itself cannot eliminate all diplonappings overnight. Rather, it should be considered as part of a concerted, international, or at least regional, approach toward the control and ultimately the prevention of such kidnappings.

Another element in a policy of minimizing the rewards is related to the legal principle examined in Chapter IV, that of political asylum. It has been emphasized that although international law generally does

[7] Elbrick, Okuchi, von Holleben and Bucher in Brazil, the First Secretary of the Swiss Embassy in Colombia, Crowley in the Dominican Republic, Holly in Guatemala, Diás Gomide in Uruguay, and Sylvester in Argentina.

[8] Sanchez in Argentina, von Spreti in Guatemala, Mitrione in Uruguay, and Elrom in Turkey. No political prisoners were released in any official exchange for Ambassador Jackson, but 106 Tupamaros escaped just prior to his release.

not recognize any *right* of extra-territorial asylum, the immunity of diplomatic premises from the territorial jurisdiction of the host state has permitted states in practice to grant such ayslum in certain cases to political refugees. These persons can only be apprehended, then, by a violation of diplomatic premises by the host governments which are highly reluctant to do so. In practice, the granting of extra-territorial asylum within foreign embassies or legations has been recognized as an established custom in Latin America where the frequencies of political upheavels and potential *coups* have led the governments concerned to regard the institution favorably as a possible future refuge for themselves. Moreover, the Havana Convention on Asylum of 1928, the Montevideo Convention on Political Asylum of 1933, and the Caracas Convention on Diplomatic Asylum of 1954 all provide in one way or another for political asylum. Since several interpretations of the first two treaties indicate that neither of them established the actual *right* of asylum, it is only the Caracas Convention (ratified by seven states) which remains in force as a legal barrier to any attempt to deny extra-territorial asylum in the diplonapping cases in Latin America. In contrast to extra-territorial asylum, territorial asylum has been regarded as a right possessed by all sovereign states. However, it is a permissive rather than an obligatory right in that the state itself determines whether it will grant or deny asylum within its territory to political refugees in any particular case.

The requirement that asylum be granted only to those prosecuted for *political* offenses is true of both extra-territorial and territorial asylum. In both cases the state granting asylum has generally assumed the right to determine whether or not a particular offense is in fact a political offense; this unilateral "right," however, has not always been recognized by the territorial state of the refugee. Moreover, it has been extremely difficult either to classify political offenses in the abstract or to determine in any particular case whether or not an offense was political in nature. Latin American practice provides no clear guidelines in the matter and international law and practice define the political offense more by negatively *excluding* certain crimes from that category than by positively including specific offenses within it. As will be seen below, terrorism has clearly been so excluded and therefore regarded as an ordinary crime meriting extradition. Under the 1971 O.A.S. Convention dealing with terrorism, diplomatic kidnappings have also been designated as common crimes and the kidnappers themselves are therefore liable to extradition.

In addition to the question of asylum for the kidnappers, there is the more complicated question as to whether asylum should be granted to any prisoners released in a diplonapping exchange. Any unilateral decisions or any international agreements to refuse to grant either territorial or extra-territorial asylum for released prisoners in the diplonapping cases, even if established only on a regional basis, could contribute substantially to a policy of minimizing the potential rewards for the diplonappers. If the kidnappers of a foreign diplomat could not expect to obtain any political asylum for the political prisoners whose release they might demand, there would be little incentive to attempt to bargain for that release in the first place. Such denial of asylum, however, runs absolutely counter to the historic practice in Latin America where, on the contrary, the concept of political asylum has had its strongest advocates.

It will be helpful at this point to briefly review the kidnapping cases again in order to determine which countries have been sought out most frequently as places of refuge for released prisoners. In the Elbrick, von Holleben, and Bucher diplonappings in Brazil the urban guerilla kidnappers specified either Mexico, Chile, or Algeria as the asylum states to which the prisoners should be sent. The fifteen prisoners released in trade for Ambassador Elbrick's freedom were granted asylum in Mexico (thirteen of them subsequently went to Cuba), the forty prisoners traded for Ambassador von Holleben were flown to Algeria whose Government granted them asylum for "humanitarian reasons," and the seventy prisoners released in exchange for Ambassador Bucher were granted asylum in Chile. In three other cases of Category Two which involved the release of political prisoners rather than the payment of ransom money, all of the specified prisoners were granted territorial asylum in Mexico after temporary extra-territorial asylum was provided for them in the Dominican Republic, Guatemala, and Brazil. In the Cross case in Canada, although no prisoners were released, the kidnappers themselves sought and were granted asylum in Cuba. Even in the other kidnappings in which diplonapper demands were not met, asylum states figured importantly in their plans for an ultimate trade. Of these, however, it was only in the case of Mitrione and Diás Gomide that a specific country was actually mentioned. The Tupamaros in Uruguay had instructed the Government to send any prisoners released in exchange for their freedom to Mexico, Peru, or Algeria.[9]

---

[9] After Mitrione's assassination, the Tupamaro ransom demand for the release of prisoners in exchange for Diás Gomide was changed to a monetary demand for one million dollars.

Because of the predominant position of Mexico as a favored state of refuge in which the diplonappers have sought potential asylum for released prisoners, it is of interest to examine recent Mexican policies toward political asylum in general. Over the past forty years several thousands of refugees have asked and been granted political asylum in Mexico; more than 10,000 came from Spain alone during the Spanish Civil War. More recently, several have been leftist revolutionaries either fleeing from their own governments or, as in the diplonapping cases, already imprisoned but released by their governments in trade for some kidnapped diplomat. Mexico has referred to the Havana treaty of 1928 as the legal basis for its consistent practice of granting political asylum and has fully abided by its provisions without exception. Although it has been noted that the 1928 Convention provides for asylum only to the extent allowed by the usages or laws of the country in which granted, Mexican custom has given it a liberal, rather than a restricted, construction.

This Mexican support for the right of political asylum can be better understood against the background of the Mexican revolution during which time Mexican leaders of all political persuasions came to value the need for and value of asylum. As a result, it is no exaggeration to regard Mexico as one of the major Latin American sanctuaries at the present time for political refugees and exiled revolutionaries. In the diplomatic kidnapping cases, however, Mexican officials have recognized the very real difficulties of distinguishing between truly political refugees and common criminals. Several of the so-called political prisoners, for example, had been incarcerated for robbing banks, shooting soldiers or policemen, and other acts of terrorism. Mexican officials have justified their granting of asylum in spite of this on the grounds that the *motivations* of such acts were political. Moreover, if asylum had been denied, the kidnapped diplomat would be the one to suffer; it was therefore granted for humanitarian reasons. Finally, several of those who were afforded asylum in the diplonapping exchanges did not remain long in the country and therefore did not come to present an internal security problem for Mexico itself.

With this in mind, it is somewhat easier to comprehend the split which has developed in Latin American ranks over the suggested policy of denying political asylum to released political prisoners as another way of minimizing the rewards for diplomatic kidnappings. At a meeting of the Permanent Council of the Organization of American States in April, 1970, Argentina 1) proposed that the Permanent Council consider the adoption of a measure condemning terrorism and kidnapping, and 2) suggested to member states the need of establishing self-imposed restrictions on the entry or transit through their territory of "criminals connected *in any way* with that type of crime . . ." [10] Anticipating objections that such action would derogate from the inter-American right of political asylum, the Argentine note maintained that asylum is essentially a humanitarian institution and therefore cannot be invoked to protect common criminals or "to further, directly or indirectly, the commission of acts of terrorism." The Argentine proposal was generally interpreted as attempting to limit asylum not only for the terrorists themselves, but also for any released political prisoners.

In the discussion that followed, the Government of Uruguay, itself plagued by the terrorist activities and kidnappings of the Tupamaros, fully supported the Argentine position and, in addition, proposed that the general topic of terrorist activities in America be placed on the agenda of the O.A.S. General Assembly Special Session to be held in June-July, 1970. Peru supported both the Argentine and Uruguayan proposals. Mexico, however, as might have been expected from that bastion of asylum, opposed any suggestion that asylum should be denied to so-called "political prisoners." Indicating that Mexico had granted political asylum to such prisoners in order to save the lives of the diplomatic hostages involved, the Mexican Ambassador to the O.A.S. quoted his Foreign Minister in explanation:

In the exceptional circumstances of the prior kidnapping of diplomats, Mexico has conceded territorial asylum moved by a humanitarian consideration to save innocent lives, and at the petition—I repeat, the petition—of the country where the kidnapping took place as well as of the country whose national was kidnapped.[11]

U.S. Ambassador John Jova [12] commended the Argentine initiative in asking the Permanent Council to consider "the difficult and anguishing problem" of kidnapping and terrorism. However, he supported the

---

[10] "Note up 68 (6005) dated April 13, 1970, from the representative of Argentina proposing that the Permanent Council consider adoption of a measure of condemnation of terrorism and kidnapping of individuals, and of organizations that resort to such means." (Italics added.) OAS/Official Records/Ser. G. - CP/Doc. 10/70 (English).

[11] Quoted by Hannifin, Rieck B., "Action within the inter-American system with regard to kidnappings of diplomats," p. 4. Report via Chief, Foreign Affairs Division, Legislative Reference Service, Library of Congress.

[12] "Statement by Joseph John Jova" in Department of State *Bulletin,* Vol. LXII, No. 1613. (May 25, 1970)

suggestion that the matter first be referred to the O.A.S. Juridical-Political Committee for its study and recommendation. Jova implied that the United States would support O.A.S. condemnation of terrorist kidnappings, but emphasized the need to distinguish between "these criminal and unpardonnable acts" and the "legitimate expression of discontent" and "desire for change" so prevalent in the Western Hemisphere. This distinction has been interpreted as "an effort to reassure the Latin Americans that the United States remains sensitive to the fact that some revolutionary activities may be necessary and just in Latin American circumstances . . ." [13]

Ambassador Jova also stated that the United States was in the midst of a very active study of the problem and of possible alternative courses of action. In an interpretive study of the O.A.S. actions with regard to the diplomatic kidnappings, a Legislative Reference Service report intimated that the United States would oppose any move to ban asylum for prisoners exchanged as ransom for kidnapped diplomats.[14] According to this analysis, the State Department supposedly doubted the value of the deterrent effect of such a policy and believed that several innocent lives might be lost in the process. This position (which would not deny asylum to prisoners once released) differs from—although it docs not necessarily directly conflict with—the U.S. position in the Mitrione case when the official State Department spokesman argued a "no ransom" policy (which would not allow the release of any prisoners in the first place). It gradually became apparent that in the O.A.S. negotiations the United States would seek to make two distinctions: 1) between terrorists and those involved in legitimate protest, and then to deny the right of asylum only to the former; and 2) between the denial of asylum to terrorists and the denial of asylum to released prisoners traded for kidnapped diplomats; in the latter case any asylum granted would be for humanitarian reasons on behalf of kidnapped victims. This position seemed to parallel that argued by the Government of Mexico.

In a compromise move the O.A.S. Council unanimously approved the "study" of the Argentine proposal by the O.A.S. Committee on Juridical-Political Affairs which met on April 20 and May 13, 1970. A Working Group was established—Argentina (Chairman), Brazil, Colombia, Chile, Guatemala, Mexico, Peru, United States, Uruguay, and Venezuela—and reported back to the full committee on May 13th. The

[13] Hannikin, *op. cit.*, p. 3.
[14] *Ibid.*, p. 8.

committee recommended to the Permanent Council of the O.A.S. a draft resolution condemning acts of terrorism and the kidnapping of individuals.[15] The draft resolution referred to the shared concern of all member states over the acts of terrorism and their unanimous repudiation of all such acts and stated "That crimes committed against representatives of foreign states, in addition to being crimes under common law, constitute serious violations, on the part of their authors, of principles that have been upheld since time immemorial; ..." The draft resolution then recommended that the Permanent Council resolve:

2. To condemn acts of terrorism and, especially, the kidnapping of persons and extortion connected with that crime as crimes against humanity.
3. To recommend to the Preparatory Committee of the General Assembly that it include on the agenda of the forthcoming special session of the Assembly a topic concerning the general action and policy of the Organization with respect to acts of terrorism and, especially, the kidnapping of persons and extortion connected with that crime.

The committee report was considered at the regular meeting of the Permanent Council on May 15, 1970, and was ultimately adopted in substance.

Before examining the 1970 summer meetings and early 1971 actions taken by the O.A.S., however, a brief analysis of terrorism as a "non-political" crime is in order. As has been pointed out, certain crimes which have been excluded from the category of political offenses may be regarded as "common crimes" which do not merit asylum and for which extradition procedures may be instituted. Terrorism is among them. In a number of actual extradition cases both homicide, as an act of terrorism, and kidnapping were not considered to be political offenses and extradition was therefore granted. As noted in Chapter IV, terrorism was also the particular target of a League of Nations draft Convention for the Prevention and Punishment of Terrorism which was drafted in 1937 but never ratified.[16] Because of its use as a precedent and several references to it as a model for recent inter-American efforts to control terrorism, some of its provisions are discussed here and summarized as follows.

[15] "Report on an action condemning acts of terrorism, the kidnapping of persons, and extortion in connection with that crime, submitted by the Committee on Juridical-Political Affairs." OAS/Official Records/Ser. G. - CP/Doc. 19/70 Rev. 1, 15 May, 1970.
[16] Reproduced in its entirety in M. O. Hudson, Ed., *International Legislation* (1941), Vol. VII, No. 499, pp. 862-878.

Article 1 defined acts of terrorism as "criminal acts directed against a State and intended or calculated to create a state of terror in the minds of particular persons, or a group of persons or the general public." Article 2 specified that all signatories would designate such acts committed in their territories and directed against another signatory as criminal offenses. Among them was included "Any wilful act causing death or grievous bodily harm or loss of liberty to: (a) Heads of States, persons exercising the prerogatives of the head of the State, . . ." and "(c) Persons charged with public functions or holding public positions when the act is directed against them in their public capacity." Finally, as particularly relevant for this survey, Article 8 provided that the terrorist offenses specified should be deemed as included "as extradition crimes" in any extradition treaties which had been or might be concluded between the signatories. Those signatories who did not make extradition conditional on the existence of a treaty also agreed under Article 8 to recognize terrorist offenses as extradition crimes as between themselves.

Although the Geneva Convention on terrorism was never ratified by enough signatories to bring it into force,[17] its definition of acts of terrorism as criminal acts directed against a state and its designation of such acts as criminal offenses which are liable to extradition have provided useful precedents for dealing with at least some of the problems raised by the diplonappings in Latin America and elsewhere today. If, for example, the risks to potential diplonappers can be increased by outlawing the kidnappings of diplomats as terrorist acts subject to extradition proceedings, the possibility of deterrence may be appreciably enhanced. Such was the purpose of the O.A.S. resolution adopted in June, 1970,[18] which not only condemned acts of terrorism and especially the kidnapping of persons as crimes against humanity, but requested the Inter-American Juridical Committee to prepare one or more draft instruments on kidnapping, extortion, and assaults against persons when such acts may have repercussions on international relations. The debates [19]

---

[17] Only three instruments of ratification or accession were required for the Convention to be registered by the Secretary-General of the League; it would have come into force for the signatories on the date of registration.

[18] "General action and policy of the organization with regard to acts of terrorism and, especially, the kidnapping of persons and extortion in connection with that crime." (Resolution adopted at the sixth plenary session, held on June 30, 1970.) AG/RES. 4 (I-E/70).

[19] Reported in the *New York Times,* June 25, 26 and 27 and August 14, 1970.

made it clear that any such treaty would declare the kidnappings of foreign diplomats to be "international crimes" not subject to the usual political immunities, such as the right of asylum.

The O.A.S. discussions dealt with all three of the prevention policy elements which have been under consideration thus far in Chapter VIII. Two of them have been mentioned in connection with the attempt to minimize the rewards as part of a policy of prevention; that is, by refusing to grant ransom demands, whether for money or for political prisoners, and also by refusing to grant political asylum to any prisoners released in a diplonapping exchange. The third element relates to the other half of the policy of prevention—the attempt to maximize the risks. One way of doing this would be to outlaw terrorism itself and to deny political asylum to all terrorists. In the O.A.S. deliberations it was generally understood that the diplomatic kidnappings were to be regarded as terrorist acts. However, there appeared to be greater agreement on the need for a concerted effort to combat terrorism by denying asylum to terrorists, than by denying asylum to released political prisoners or by refusing ransom demands for their release in the first place. Thus, when Brazil urged a "hard-line" policy in which all governments would agree not to provide asylum to any political prisoners freed as ransom for kidnapped victims, Mexico and Chile argued that this would infringe on the Latin American "principle" of political asylum. However, Argentina, Uruguay, Paraguay and Guatemala pledged not to make any "deals" with kidnappers, no matter what the cost in human lives.

The O.A.S. resolution finally adopted was originally proposed by Brazil as a draft resolution to exclude terrorists from the right of political asylum. As mentioned, there was less opposition to this move than to the denial of asylum for released political prisoners. Nonetheless, in its demands that terrorists be treated as common criminals and so be excluded from the right of political sanctuary and in its call for a drastic revision within ninety days of the Havana Convention of 1928 and other judicial instruments on political asylum, the resolution provoked a good deal of controversy. As in the case of the earlier attempt to deny asylum to political prisoners, it was opposed by the Governments of both Mexico and Chile who argued that it was too extreme. (It should be noted that both Mexico and Chile had been particularly specified in the diplonapping cases as possible refuges for purposes of political asylum and that Mexico, though not Chile, has ratified both the 1928 Havana Convention on Asylum and the 1954 Caracas Convention on Diplomatic Asylum. Interestingly, Brazil has also ratified both documents, although

Argentina has ratified neither. Argentina, however, is one of the five signatories of an 1889 treaty providing for asylum, which is still in force.)

At this point the United States assumed a position in favor of the Brazilian proposal for the Juridical Committee to develop "a new international agreement) to counter terrorism by the denial of political asylum to any person involved in terrorist acts. Attending the meeting in person, U.S. Secretary of State William Rogers stated: "We live in an era of increasing violence as a mode of dissent. None of our countries is immune to it." Then, echoing earlier U.S. statements, he continued, "In dealing with the problem we must be most careful to distinguish between criminal acts of terrorism and legitimate expressions of discontent." [20] He also suggested that the O.A.S. Assembly should initiate steps to prepare "a new international agreement defining these acts as international crimes and establishing appropriate measures to deal with them." It was reported that the United States had in mind an agreement which would strengthen the inter-American system's ability to prevent violence and to respond more uniformly to emergency situations; such response would be enhanced by closer exchanges of information on subversion in the hemisphere, coordination of military action to protect foreign nationals threatened by violence in any of the member states, and an appeal to other states for greater attention to the use of their territory for terrorist plots.[21] These provisions in modified form were ultimately included in Article 8 of the O.A.S. Convention which was adopted.

The Inter-American Juridical Committee completed a draft treaty on terrorism and kidnapping in late September, 1970. It was reported that seven representatives on the committee had voted for the draft (Argentina, Brazil, Guatemala, Nicaragua, Trinidad, the United States, and Uruguay), two had voted against it (Chile and Peru), and two had abstained (Colombia and Mexico).[22] When the draft treaty was submitted for discussion by the O.A.S. foreign ministers,[23] a split developed between six "hard-line" states [24] (who sought a broad convention based on the draft itself which would outlaw *all* political terrorism, including kid-

---

[20] Quoted in the *New York Times,* June 27, 1970.

[21] Reported in *ibid.,* June 27, 1970.

[22] *Ibid.,* September 28, 1970.

[23] The following account is based on reports in the *New York Times,* February 2 and 3, 1971, and in *The Milwaukee Journal,* February 2 and 3, 1971.

[24] Argentina, Brazil, Ecuador, Guatemala, Haiti, and Paraguay.

napping, and would provide for the extradition of all those accused of such terrorism) and a majority of the seventeen other states (who preferred a more restricted treaty which would only outlaw the kidnapping of foreign officials and diplomats). After a walk-out by the six, the remaining delegations voted 13 to 1, with 2 abstentions to approve the more restricted treaty.[25]

The voting alignments clearly reflected the ideological divisions between the militarist regimes which favored strong anti-terrorist measures and the leftist regimes which opposed any treaty at all. In between the two extremes were those who favored the treaty as finally adopted by the General Assembly of the O.A.S. on February 2, 1971. The position of those opposed to any convention at all was voiced by the delegate from Chile who maintained that the proposed convention violated the sovereignties of the Latin American states. He argued that the "roots of violence" responsible for terrorism arose from the misery in which much of Latin America continued to live; in dealing with terrorism in legal terms, the convention had ignored this aspect of the problem. It should be noted that the voting also reflected the concerns of those governments most bedeviled by terrorist activities in their own territories who either voted with the majority or boycotted the meeting in the hope of securing an even stronger document.

The most important articles of the approved *"CONVENTION TO PREVENT AND PUNISH THE ACTS OF TERRORISM TAKING THE FORM OF CRIMES AGAINST PERSONS AND RELATED EXTORTION THAT ARE OF INTERNATIONAL SIGNIFICANCE"*[26] specified:

Article 1

The contracting states undertake to cooperate among themselves by taking all the measures that they may consider effective, under their own laws, and especially those established in this convention, to prevent and punish acts of terrorism, especially kidnapping, murder, and other assaults against the life or physical integrity of those persons

---

[25] Bolivia and Peru abstained; Chile cast the negative vote.

[26] CONVENTION TO PREVENT AND PUNISH THE ACTS OF TERRORISM TAKING THE FORM OF CRIMES AGAINST PERSONS AND RELATED EXTORTION THAT ARE OF INTERNATIONAL SIGNIFICANCE. OAS/OFFICIAL RECORDS/Ser. P/ENGLISH-AG/doc. 88 rev. 1 corr. 1, 2 February 1971.

to whom the state has the duty according to international law to give special protection, as well as extortion in connection with those crimes.

Article 2

For the purposes of this convention, kidnapping, murder, and other assaults against the life or personal integrity of those persons to whom the state has the duty to give special protection according to international law, as well as extortion in connection with those crimes, shall be considered common crimes of international significance, regardless of motive.

Article 3

Persons who have been charged or convicted for any of the crimes referred to in Article 2 of this convention shall be subject to extradition under the provisions of the extradition treaties in force between the parties or, in the case of states that do not make extradition dependent on the existence of a treaty, in accordance with their own laws.

In any case, it is the exclusive responsibility of the state under whose jurisdiction or protection such persons are located to determine the nature of the acts and decide whether the standards of this convention are applicable.

It should be noted that although Article 1 states that the parties will take measures under their own laws to prevent and punish acts of terrorism, especially kidnapping (thus implying that measures should be taken against other acts of terrorism as well), Articles 2 and 3, which are the operative articles in terms of *international* action, only refer to kidnapping, murder, and assaults against those toward whom states have the obligation of special protection. Such acts of terrorism are declared to be common crimes and those charged or convicted of them are subject to extradition. In addition to these central ideas, Article 8 of the Convention stated that the parties to it would also: take all measures within their power to prevent and impede the preparation within their own territories of the specified crimes which might be carried out in the territory of another contracting state, exchange information and consider other effective administrative measures to protect diplomats, and include the criminal acts specified in their own penal laws, if not already so included.

At the same session at which it adopted the Convention, the O.A.S. General Assembly also instructed the Permanent Council [27] to study those matters pertaining to "progressive international cooperation" in the prevention and punishment of acts of terrorism, especially kidnapping, that are of international significance and which were not covered by the Convention itself or by other treaties. The Assembly suggested that member states examine "with nonmember states interested in this question" the possibility of their adherence to the Convention or the consideration of the adoption of a world convention on the subject.

In a statement to the Assembly on January 27th on behalf of the U.S. Secretary of State,[28] Under Secretary Irwin had stressed the U.S. concern for achieving a convention with "strong enforcement provisions" and real prospects for winning wide support both in the O.A.S. and elsewhere. Because of this and the legal and political difficulties involved in reaching agreement on a definition of terrorism in general, the U.S. delegation had favored focusing on the kidnappings and other terrorist acts against foreign officials—a subject upon which there was more general accord. The United States maintained that such a convention should establish effective enforcement procedures to bring the violators to judgment and that it should include ". . . the obligation to seek out offenders, to detain them, and to extradite or submit them for prosecution."

The United States voted with the majority in favor of the Convention, and in a statement by the U.S. Secretary of State, as delivered by Ambassador Jova, the U.S. position was amplified.[29] The statement stressed the fact that although the majority had opted for a more "specific convention" than the six had wanted, this was only a first step; it expressed the hope that all member states would ultimately subscribe

[27] INSTRUCTION TO THE PERMANENT COUNCIL OF THE ORGANIZA-TION TO STUDY MATTERS PERTAINING TO TERRORISM, ASSAULTS AGAINST PERSONS, AND EXTORTION IN CONNECTION WITH THOSE CRIMES. (Resolution approved by the General Assembly at the fifth plenary session, held on February 2, 1971.) OAS/OFFICIAL RECORDS/Ser. P/ENGLISH-AG/RES. 24 (III-E/71), 2 February, 1971. Not ratified by any states as of 11/1/72.

[28] Statement by the Secretary of State at the O.A.S. General Assembly, January 27, 1971. (Delivered before the Assembly by Under Secretary Irwin.) Department of State *Bulletin,* Vol. LXIV, No. 1652. (February 22, 1971.)

[29] Statement by the Secretary of State at the Final Plenary Session of the O.A.S. General Assembly, February 2, 1971. (As delivered by Ambassador Joseph John Jova, U.S. Representative to the O.A.S.) *Ibid.*

to the Convention and participate in the next steps to cope with "the general problem of terrorism." The United States also hoped that states outside the hemisphere would accede to the Convention or, if not, would recognize in their own practice the principles it articulated. In explaining the U.S. interpretation of Article 2, the statement maintained that Assembly discussions had clearly reflected the general understanding that it applied "not only to diplomatic agents, consular officers, and members of their families, but also to other officials of foreign governments and officials of public international organizations."

In a news briefing [30] on February 3, 1971, a State Department spokesman reiterated U.S. concern over the voting split in the O.A.S. Stating that the United States was not indifferent to other acts of terrorism, besides the kidnappings, he repeated the hope that the six would accede to the Convention and, building on that basis, collaborate in the future development of international law in that area. The spokesman stated: "This convention makes a major contribution to international law. It is the first time that any international agreement has specified that the murder or kidnapping of representatives of states are not to be considered as political offenses whose perpetrators are sheltered by asylum." He also mentioned that the Convention was open to states outside the Hemisphere and that the United States hoped that many would accede to it; a general acceptance of such principles by the international community could be a "moral deterrent" to this kind of crime.

Before returning to an analysis of the overall strategy of deterrence outlined at the beginning of this chapter, a few paragraphs should be devoted to the other international organizations which have considered the diplomatic kidnappings. In May, 1970, the Government of the Netherlands brought the matter of the protection and inviolability of diplomatic agents to the attention of the President of the Security Council. In a letter [31] stating that diplomatic immunity and inviolability has been clearly established by the rules of international law, the Netherlands maintained that the increasing number of attacks on diplomats was "a cause of alarm" since such incidents could endanger friendly relations between states and even lead to situations which might give rise to a dispute which as such could endanger international peace and

---

[30] Transcript of Press, Radio and Television News Briefing (Wednesday, February 3, 1971). Department of State, DPC 24. Also quoted in *ibid.*

[31] United Nations Office of Public Information, *U.N. Monthly Chronicle*, Vol. VIII, No. 2 (December, 1971), p. 149.

security. The note expressed the hope that the President would inform the members of the Security Council of these concerns. Although the letter appears in U.N. records, the matter was not discussed in any detail either in the Security Council or in the General Assembly and the United Nations took no immediate action on it.

In the autumn meetings of the 26th General Assembly in 1971,[32] however, the Assembly discussed the kidnapping of diplomats and requested the International Law Commission to study the protection and inviolability of diplomatic agents and other persons entitled to special protection under international law. The Commission was also requested to prepare a set of draft articles dealing with offenses committed against diplomats and to submit them to the General Assembly at the earliest possible date considered appropriate by the Commission. The Assembly asked the Secretary-General to invite comments from member states on "protection of diplomats" before April 1, 1972, and to submit them to the next session of the International Law Commission to be held in Geneva in May.[33]

In December, 1970, the Council of Europe in Strasbourg did consider the question of the "Protection of Members of Diplomatic Missions and Consular Posts." [34] Its Committee of Ministers declared that the acts of violence perpetrated against such members constituted "grave violations" of the most sacred international traditions and it unanimously condemned all attacks on the lives and persons of diplomatic and consular personnel and, in particular, the diplomatic kidnappings. In its resolution the Committee also recommended that the governments of member states: 1) survey the security measures in force for the protection of diplomats and, whenever necessary, reinforce them, 2) examine the extent to which their national laws provide for the severe punishment of those guilty of attacks on the lives and persons of diplomats, and 3) ensure among themselves close cooperation in matters of protection of diplomats against such attacks. The Committee decision was regarded as a "considered protest" against the increase in assaults on diplomats

[32] The Draft Articles appear at the end of this book as Appendix IV.

[33] Letter dated 5 May 1970 from the Permanent Representative of the Netherlands to the United Nations. Addressed to the President of the Security Council. United Nations Security Council - S/9789. 12 May, 1970.

[34] "Protection of Members of Diplomatic Missions and Consular Posts." Council of Europe, Committee of Ministers, Resolution (70) 51. (Adopted by the Ministers on 11 December 1970).

and related incidents and as an attempt to help mobilize public opinion.[35]

Although the increase of terrorism and diplomatic kidnappings have thus become a matter of general international concern, it is only the O.A.S. Convention of 1971 which has emerged as an international treaty specifically condemning and outlawing the diplomatic kidnappings as common crimes whose perpetrators are subject to extradition procedures. Even its most enthusiastic supporters, however, would not argue that in itself such a treaty can totally prevent the terrorist attempts at diplonapping. It is especially important in this regard to recall some of the implicit assumptions made at the beginning of this section. In particular, it was stated that the policy of deterrence assumes that the diplonappers are "rational" and "will weigh the actual risks involved against the potential rewards" in any particular case. The fact that the diplonappings have taken place in an atmosphere of terrorism and have been used as a *technique* of terrorism calls for further examination of these assumptions.

It also calls for an assessment of the diplonappers' motives. If the diplonappers are primarily motivated by the prospect of reward—either in ransom money or in freed political prisoners—and if that potential reward is removed, then their incentive will be correspondingly reduced or removed. Thus, if a policy of "no ransom" were in fact uniformly adopted by the Latin American states and others, by unilateral declarations or by multilateral treaty, and if that policy were bolstered by a general agreement not to provide asylum for any political prisoners who might be released, then the rewards for diplonapping would be slight indeed. Equally true, if the diplonappers are, in fact, "rational" in assessing the risks involved and if those risks are maximized, then again deterrence may work. This is an argument for the denial of political asylum to the terrorists themselves and part of the rational underlying the O.A.S. Convention.

A somewhat different picture emerges, however, if one does not necessarily accept the complete rationality of the terrorists in the balancing of rewards versus risks *or* if one assumes a slightly different or additional motivation for their actions. Following this line of reasoning just briefly, it is entirely possible that although the diplonappers are quite ready to accept money and/or the exchange of prisoners as "an extra dividend" or even as a welcome reward, they are not motivated entirely or even primarily by that reward in and of itself. Since most

---

[35] *London Times,* December 12, 1970.

of the diplonappers are highly dedicated revolutionaries or members of organized terrorist bands they may be more concerned with the turmoil they can create and the insecurity they can foster in their attempt to overthrow the established government, than with any particular sum of money or any specified number of imprisoned colleagues. Their motivation in such a scenario arises as much from the desire to instigate terror as to reap rewards.

If this portrait of the diplonappers and their motivation depicts them accurately, then it is obvious that a strategy of deterrence and prevention will depend as much on a policy of maximizing the risks as on one of minimizing the rewards, since "the rewards" in the case of terrorists are to be found in the consummation of the terrorist acts themselves and in the atmosphere of terror which they create. The remaining question, then, is what measures of protection and security can be taken to prevent the success of diplonapping attempts and, ultimately, to deter them altogether. The question is an obvious one and the general security steps which might be taken (and which have been taken) are equally obvious. What is more difficult to ascertain are the details of such measures and whether, since their institution, they have been successful. Not only is there very little available concerning this in the public record,[36] but even unofficial "off-the-record" conversations with diplomats and State Department personnel in Washington have been of limited value.

Several diplonapping attempts have been made when the diplomatic target is traveling by auto, entering his auto, or leaving it—in other words, outside of the embassy itself and outside the official residence, if there is one. One method of guarding against a possible kidnapping during transit is, of course, an increase in the use and number of bodyguards. Many diplomats now have permanent bodyguards; others have guards ride with them in their limousine or have them follow in trailing vehicles. The continual presence of bodyguards, however, can seriously inhibit an ambassador in the normal performance of his daily tasks and in his contacts with the local citizenry. Moreover, such measures have not greatly deterred the kidnappers in practice, and, as evidenced in the von Holleben kidnapping in Brazil, did not prevent the diplonapping

---

[36] A concise unofficial survey of possible protective measures may be found in the *New York Times,* August 14, 1970. Some of the following is based on that article. Another more personal account on how security measures affect the life style of the American diplomat abroad may be found in the *Wall Street Journal,* January 14, 1971.

when attempted. As can be seen from the case studies, the diplonappers usually carry out their raids in groups of four to six men, thus out-numbering any modest deployment of bodyguards. Moreover, any U.S. demands for tighter security measures to be taken by the Latin American governments may be counter-productive; thus, in April, 1970, the U.S. Ambassador to Brazil was criticized for publicly expressing concern for the safety of U.S. diplomats in Brazil.[37]

Other measures to protect diplomats abroad which have been suggested include the reduction in size of embassy and consulate staffs, so reducing the size of the target. This has already been done in several overseas missions, particularly in Uruguay where the Mitrione/Diás Gomide/Fly/Jackson quartette of diplonappings has set the teeth of foreign emissaries on thin edge. Officials of the Brazilian Ambassy, for example, sent home certain members of their own families whom they regarded as potential kidnapping targets.[38] Although children have not yet been selected as targets, security precautions have also been set up on a family basis and the children of American diplomats overseas are heavily guarded. Another possible preventive technique is to drastically cut unnecessary travel as well as to thicken the secrecy veil in planning any essential trips. United States embassies in Latin America have issued directives to their staff and employees to avoid talking even to close friends and associates about travel plans. Lunching out has been severely curtailed and many diplomats content themselves with sandwiches at their desks. Moreover, work hours have been switched and staggered on a daily basis to prevent routine comings and goings which are notice-able and therefore vulnerable to possible kidnappings.

Another travel practice recently instituted is to schedule embassy limousine with new oversize rear-view mirrors for travel in convoys, picking up entire staffs from their homes, delivering them to the mission, and returning them home after work. A concomitant problem created by this effort, however, arises from the fact that most of the diplonappings have occurred and are likely to occur in urban areas where the heavy traffic can easily separate convoy groupings. The suggestion to follow alternate routes to and from the embassy has also been countered by the observation that most of the kidnappings have actually taken place close to either end of the route—at or near the embassy or the home itself. A somewhat more subtle method, and perhaps possessing more

[37] Reported in *U.S. News and World Report,* April 20, 1970.
[38] Reported in the *New York Times,* August 14, 1970.

potential because of its simplicity, has been for embassy staff members to remove their diplomatic license plates from their cars and in some cases even to use smaller and less ostentatious vehicles for their travel. Although some agents carry arms and, as noted in Chapter V, the United States even ordered its diplomats in certain areas of Southeast Asia to carry guns, this practice has been regarded by some as extremely dangerous and even provocative to the diplonappers.

Since United States dilpomatic representatives have frequently served as the targets of kidnapping attempts, the U.S. Government has been particularly concerned with possible ways of increasing security and counteracting terrorism. The State Department, for example, asked Congress in June, (1970, for a supplemental appropriation of $1.9 million and 43 additional personnel [39] to strengthen and improve the security for overseas embassy staff members, with an emphasis upon their personal protection. The State Department maintained that it expected more assassinations and kidnappings of American diplomats abroad and requested both money and manpower to attempt to prevent and counter them. Specifically, it was reported, the department wanted to organize "emergency action teams," including a Navy Seabee armor expert, which could be deployed quickly to any trouble spots. It also asked for a fleet of heavily armored vehicles, increased Marine guards at U.S. embassies, and additional money to hire more local guards.[40]

The State Department was almost brutally frank in its request for the funds which stated:

At present it is beyond the Department of State's capability to provide maximum security to our ambassadors and other high ranking U.S. officials. The threat of personal attack is particularly acute in certain areas of the world.[41]

This supplemental request was made before the Committee on Appropriations and although a major portion regarding specific measures of protection was deleted when the Committee went off the record, enough remains in the hearings to provide at least a few insights into current governmental thinking. The Deputy Under Secretary of State for

---

[39] Senate Hearings, Committee on Appropriations: "State, Justice, Commerce, the Judiciary, and Related Agencies Appropriations" (H.R. 17575 - 91st Congress, Second Session - Fiscal Year 1971), pp. 411-14. Although press releases referred to a request for $1.25 million, Deputy Under Secretary of State, William B. Macomber, Jr., requested $1.9 million in the Committee hearings.

[40] UPI report in *The Milwaukee Journal*, August 21, 1970.

[41] Reported in *ibid*.

Administration, William B. Macomber, testified. Having referred to the assassination of Ambassador John Gordon Mein in Guatemala and the kidnapping of Ambassador Elbrick in Brazil, Mr. Macomber continued:

We believe it is imperative to provide a greater measure of protection for our people and their families in many countries.

The proposal you now have before you for consideration would provide needed additional protection. Our plan for utilization of these security measures and equipment is a flexible one that would permit assignment of personnel and equipment where the threats are the greatest.[42]

The Deputy Under Seretary then indicated that it was the assessment of the Department of State that the problem of kidnapping and violence to U.S. officials and their families overseas was "a growing problem" and one that would have to be dealt with for quite some time. In attempting to deal with it, Macomber said, there were three different approaches which could be followed:

First, we can try to deal with it in international bodies and through the international community.

Second, we can try to deal with it in our dealings with the specific countries concerned.

Third, we can try to deal with it through providing physical security protection to our people on the ground.[43]

Presumably all three would be followed simultaneously. The activities of the United States in the deliberations of the Organization of American States have already been mentioned and it can also be assumed that direct bilateral negotiations and planning have taken place between U.S. officials and the representatives of various Latin American countries. The specifics of Point Three—"providing physical security protection" to U.S. personnel on the spot are not published, however, for at this point the Committee went off the record. The only details available are the newspaper reports about "emergency action teams," mentioned above.

The Committee Hearings provide information on only two other aspects of United States strategies in this matter of security measures. First, the request for 43 new positions (10 Americans and 33 local persons) was presumably made for security officers and for bodyguards. In the testimony regarding those positions, Mr. Macomber indicated that the State Department then had full-time security officers in nineteen countries; it planned to place them in seven additional countries. Although

---

[42] Senate Hearings, Committee on Appropriations: *op. cit.*, p. 412.
[43] *Ibid.*

none of the countries was specified, UPI indicated that it had learned that a number of them were in Latin America, which surmise is hardly surprising. Macomber stated that he anticipated no opposition to the program or no problem with the security forces of host countries; on the contrary, they would probably welcome the measures. The second bit of information gleaned from the hearings referred to the request for $76,000 for in-country air travel for the U.S. Ambassador to Brazil. The State Department argued that travel by car through a country as large as Brazil with two capitals and seven U.S. consulates was simply too dangerous. Air travel could be provided by U.S. military aircraft since commercial flying would be subject to the possibility of air hijackings.

Hearings dealing with the security of U.S. diplomats abroad were also held before the Subcommittee on Inter-American Affairs of the House Foreign Affairs Committee on April 27, 1970.[44] However, since the open hearings lasted only from 2:25 P.M. until 2:45 P.M., when the subcommittee adjourned to continue later in executive session, it is understandable, though regrettable, that the published report is contained within only ten pages! The chairman set a tone of urgency in his introductory remarks:

The rising incidence of kidnapings of diplomatic personnel has created a crisis for the conduct of normal relations between the countries of this hemisphere. Unless something is done to remedy this situation, international relations may come to be dictated by the whims and self-designated necessities of guerrillas, terrorists, and other extreme radical elements.

He then indicated that the subcommittee was concerned both with the safety of U.S. diplomats abroad and with the general threat posed to the conduct of international relations by the diplomatic kidnappings and assassinations. Deputy Under Secretary of State for Administration, William B. Macomber, again testified for the State Department but in effect simply provided the subcommittee with a briefing memorandum on the Argentine initiative at the O.A.S. and the U.S. response to it.[45]

The Deputy Assistant Secretary of State for Inter-American Affairs, Robert A. Hurwitch, also testified, but his formal remarks were also directed primarily to the briefing memorandum. In response to all

---

[44] "Safety of U.S. Diplomats." Hearings before the Subcommittee on Inter-American Affairs of the Committee on Foreign Affairs, HR 91st Congress, 2nd Session. (April 27, 1970)

[45] Discussed above, pp. 141-44.

detailed questions of specific policy steps which the U.S. had taken or might take, both Macomber and Hurwitch responded that they would deal with such questions in executive session; all of the following, for example, were put off to the executive session: Was there any "common pattern" to the kidnappings? What "specific steps" had the U.S. taken? Had there been any kidnapping threats to foreign diplomats stationed in the U.S.? Who was behind the kidnappings—internal terrorists or external political forces? What preventive measures are generally being taken by governments?

In explanation of this apparent reticence to discuss these matters more openly, Mr. Macomber had stated his own reservations quite directly at the opening of the hearing:

We have given a great deal of attention, Mr. Chairman, to how best to deal with this problem, focusing on how we can increase the risks to potential kidnapers, and reduce the rewards to potential kidnapers. But, frankly, all the things that we have examined and have underway to help accomplish these objectives are the kind that are not best discussed in public, and I regret very much to say that if we are going to have a meaningful discussion of them, I am afraid that I would have to ask to go into executive session.

At the end of the meeting he made his point more dramatically when he said, ". . . I am terribly conscious that anything I could say here could wind up losing a life." Probably the most that came out of the hearings was Macomber's emphasis upon a policy that would "reduce the rewards" and "increase the risks"—a policy which essentially has been the theme of much of this chapter. In addition, he agreed that actions designed to carry out such a policy could be undertaken unilaterally, bilaterally, and multilaterally. The United States was currently directing its multilateral efforts through the O.A.S. "before going to other arenas, or other types of proposals."

In August, 1970, the Senate also became involved in discussing the diplomatic kidnappings when Senator Byrd of West Virginia introduced a Resolution [46] expressing the sense of the Senate that the President should take such steps as might be necessary to secure at the earliest practicable time bilateral or multilateral agreements on measures which might be taken to prevent and punish any threats or acts unlawfully endangering the life or freedom of foreign officials, members of international organizations, or their families. Under such agreements, signatory states would agree: to treat all such officials with due respect and to take all

[46] S. Res. 454. *Congressional Record-Senate,* S 14047-14050. (August 24, 1970)

appropriate steps to prevent such threats or acts; to apprehend, prosecute or extradite any person who commits or threatens to commit such acts; to refuse to grant asylum or to capture and to extradite any person whose release from the custody of another state had been achieved by such threats; to withold formal recognition of any government formed by any group which participated in such threats or acts; and to undertake other appropriate measures to deter similar actions in the future. The Resolution was referred to the Committee on Foreign Relations which in turn referred it to the Department of State for comment. No action was taken and the measure died in committee.

As has been mentioned above, American interest in diplomatic security has not been limited to the need to establish and increase security provisions for U.S. personnel overseas, however. Equally important, and at present both a current worry and a potential problem, is the provision and insurance of security for foreign representatives stationed in the United States, either in embassies or legations in Washington or accredited to the United Nations in New York. The State Department's security office has been particularly concerned by the increasing number of robberies, muggings and assaults against diplomatic envoys which have paralleled the rising crime rate in general and the bombings and bomb threats, in particular, throughout the country's larger cities. Although recent crimes of this nature against foreign diplomats have apparently lacked political motivation, the possibility that the Latin American style diplonappings and terrorist tactics might be imported into the United States has seriously worried State Department security officers. In 1971, the speculation and uncertain evidence surrounding the alleged plot to kidnap presidential advisor Henry Kissinger did little to alleviate their anxieties. State Department spokesman have even admitted the possibility of such "unthinkable incidents" as the von Spreti affair occurring in the United States; yet no detailed contingency plan for dealing with such an incident has been reported.

Some security precautions have already been instituted, however, partly in response to demands from at least fifty countries with missions in Washington who had requested stronger security measures. (There are over 114 embassies in Washington, including 23 representing Latin American countries.) As of early August, 1970, a new police force, the Executive Protective Service, was created to protect foreign embassies and resident diplomats in the capital. It consists of 850 men, 250 of whom were previously assigned to the White House Police Force and an additional 600 men; the new force will operate as the Foreign Missions

Division of the Secret Service. Previously, the Washington Metropolitan Police had given special attention to embassy security but were also responsible for the control of all city crime. The Executive Protective Service is now able to devote full time to protection and security for foreign diplomats as well as for the White House.[47]

It was reported that about sixty EPS officers would patrol streets in the areas where embassies and legations are located, including four suburban neighborhoods; Metropolitan Police would continue to patrol other areas of the capital. Some EPS officers also stand guard at potential trouble spots where a 24-hour guard has been requested. After the Mitrione diplonapping, for example, the Executive Protective Service posted a 24-hour guard at the Uruguayan chancery in Washington. In addition, it is anticipated that in some cases EPS officers may accompany foreign diplomats to other parts of the United States when they travel there on state visits. The newly appointed head of the EPS described its role as preventive. The 14-week training session for new officers includes first aid, special driver training, arrest procedures, city geography, and information on narcotics and other dangerous drugs. It appears that the course was designed to deal both with the "normal" crimes of any large city and with the possibility of diplomatic kidnappings. Since the institution of the EPS in August, 1970, through early 1971, reported crime at foreign embassies in Washington has been drastically reduced.[48] It would not be surprising if other states, particularly in Latin America, adopted similar security precautions in the future. In addition to the EPS, a new U.S. Secret Service unit was formed in early 1971 to protect foreign dignitaries visiting the United States.[49] Little is known about its *modus operandi.*

Despite such unilateral security measures taken by any one or more states, the prevention of terrorism in general or, more accurately, its control cannot be accomplished quickly, easily, or with any single policy recommendation. A *New York Times* article on the diplonappings, entitled "Political Kidnappings Spread Insecurity Through Latin America," was even gloomier in its analysis.[50] Stating that the spread of

[47] The preceding account is based on reports in the *New York Times,* August 20, 1970, and *The Milwaukee Journal,* August 24, 1970. About 250 men will continue to guard the White House and adjacent Executive Office. The 600 additional men will assume responsibility for foreign embassies and ambassadorial residences.
[48] Reported in *The Milwaukee Journal,* February 11, 1971.
[49] *Ibid.,* February 28, 1971.
[50] *New York Times,* August 14, 1970.

political kidnappings had forced foreign embassies in Latin America to worry more about the security of their own staff than about international relations, the article cited the "nearly unanimous opinion" of officials that no real solution is likely to be found short of eleminating all terrorists. This rather pessimistic conclusion was basesd on the assessment that Latin American guerillas of all ideologies—many of them Marxist or quasi-Marxist—have decided that kidnapping is a highly effective weapon in a revolutionary "war" usually waged against vastly superior military and police forces. Therefore, although political kidnappings are not entirely new to Latin America, they have recently become an increasingly common practice. As concluded in Chapter I, diplonappings, as a technique of terrorism, fit in with the concept of urban guerilla warfare as opposed to the countryside campaigns which have declined since the semi-failure in Bolivia of the rural guerilla bands led by Ché Guevara. The fact that the Tupamaros in Uruguay, the Rebel Armed Forces in Guatemala, and the Brazilian A.L.N. are all urban guerilla groups confirms this particular contention.

In addition to their long-term revolutionary goals, the urban terrorists' short-term objectives aim to embarrass and weaken their domestic governments and to strain relations between them and other countries. In this they have succeeded. Along with the highly publicized ransom rewards of freed prisoners and monetary payments, terrorist activities have resulted in: a severe reduction in the diplomatic relations between the Federal Republic of Germany and Guatemala; extensive governmental reprisals in terms of tightened security and/or periodic suspensions of civil rights in Argentina, Brazil, Canada, Colombia, the Dominican Republic, Guatemala, Turkey, and Uruguay; security precautions in overseas U.S. embassies which have restricted the movement of diplomats in some cases so much as to interfere with their normal duties;[51] Brazilian pique and irritation with the refusal of Uruguay to release any prisoners in exchange for a Brazilian consul; numerous and widespread mass media publication and distribution of guerilla manifestos and propaganda statements; and the split over asylum and no asylum policies toward terrorists which developed in the O.A.S. deliberations on the 1971 Convention.

Because of the absolute increase and spread of the diplomatic kidnappings and their legal, political, and moral implications not only for the individual states directly affected, but for the entire world community,

[51] Reported in *U.S. News and World Report,* April 20, 1970.

it is obvious that they have become a serious international problem which will require international efforts for its solution. The institution of unilateral national security precautions will be necessary but not sufficient to deal with the mounting number of both attempted and successful diplonappings—to say nothing of the parallel problem of sky-jackings—which have taken place over the past five years. In addition, the O.A.S. Convention to outlaw the diplomatic kidnappings as common crimes and to deny the sanctuary of political asylum to the kidnappers was not only highly desirable, but should be expanded to include other states or be emulated by them. Equally effective, though difficult of achievement, would be a Latin American regional treaty or even a more universal agreement to refuse to grant asylum to any political prisoners who might be released in exchange for kidnapped diplomats. Finally, although a no ransom policy is vulnerable to charges that it callously ignores the plight of the diplomatic hostage, if it were followed consistently by all concerned, it could contribute over the long run to a general strategy of deterrence. That strategy has been advocated here both to minimize the rewards and to maximize the risks which may be expected by potential kidnappers. It is not a panacea which will eradicate the causes of revolutionary violence; but it may present a rational policy to prevent or to control one manifestation of that violence—diplomatic kidnappings as a technique of urban terrorism.

SUMMARY

Any conclusions on a political and legal problem of such immediate concern as the diplomatic kidnappings must be tentative at best. The conclusions offered within these pages should be so regarded. For purposes of summary, the author would like to utilize a technique which has proved successful through some fourteen years of thinking and teaching about international relations at the university level. With the purpose of provoking students to regard international problems—despite all their complexities and ambiguities—in a logical manner and with a view to producing policy-oriented recommendations, they have frequently been urged to consider and to attempt to answer the following questions: What is the problem? Which states and international organizations are involved and what policies have they pursued? What tentative theories may be applied? What alternative or additional policies should be considered? Which recommendations should be made?

The problem arises from the diplomatic kidnappings which have been perpetrated by revolutionary terrorists variously motivated by the possibility of ransom money or freedom for political prisoners and by the desire to embarrass and harass the government in power, to strain its diplomatic relations with other states, and/or to create an atmsophere of instability and terror. Legally, the diplonappings infringe upon the personal inviolability, privileges and immunities of diplomatic representatives and call into operation the indirect responsibility of states to provide special protection for them and to prevent such violations. Politically, the diplonappings impair the normal conduct and flow of international diplomacy and diplomatic contacts between states upon which amicable and regularized international relations rest. Morally, they are repugnant to such human concepts as the freedom and dignity of life and liberty, the rule of law and order, and the belief in "fair play."

All states are affected by the diplonappings—either indirectly or directly. Indirectly, the international community at large can only suffer from terrorist tactics which not only totally disregard any precepts of international law, but disrupt the very foundations of international intercourse. Directly, all states are equally susceptible to the actual or potential technique of diplonapping. In the recent cases of diplomatic kidnappings, the Latin American states, the United States and Canada, and some of the European powers as well as the Organization of American States have been most directly involved. In terms of policies pursued, all of these states have followed similar preventive policies of verbal denunciation and attempted security measures. Once a kidnapping has occurred, however, their policies have diverged. European and United States practice has tended to disavow any legal right of extra-territorial political asylum; Latin American states in contrast have all granted extra-territorial asylum in practice and some have even regarded it as part of regional legal custom. There is also a division between the Latin American states themselves regarding the granting of ransom demands, some regularly acceding to such demands and others refusing to meet them. More recently, the United States has informally favored a "no ransom" policy.

As to tentative theories, Chapter VIII has set forth in some detail the idea of combatting the diplonappings by concerted preventive policies involving the minimization of potential rewards and the maximization of potential risks. Such a policy of deterrence is at least partly dependent upon the assumption that the diplonappers are in fact motivated by the desire for such rewards as ransom money or freed political prisoners who may count on assured asylum in friendly states. If they are so motivated, then the theory remains valid: That is, if ransom will be denied or if the desired asylum will not be granted, there will be no rewards and no reason to attempt a kidnapping. If, however, the primary motivation is the promulgation of terrorism itself, then a policy of minimizing "rewards" which are not actually significant to the diplonappers can hardly serve as an effective deterrent. The other half of the theory—that of increasing the risks—is not liable to the same criticism and remains essentially valid. Thus, the provision of extradition for diplomatic kidnappers and any security measures designed to increase diplomatic protection can only be salutary as part of a preventive policy.

Finally, in light of the problem described, the states and organizations involved, the policies pursued by them, and the theory proferred above, what alternative or additional policies can be recommended? Despite the limitations mentioned in any attempt to deter by minimizing rewards, a consistent, region-wide policy of "no ransom" coupled with a denial of asylum to released political prisoners appears to be a better alternative than continued accession to all demands. Success breeds emulation, and if "diplonapping" comes to be regarded as a foolproof technique, it is likely to be tried even more in the future than it has been in the past. This is especially true if all released prisoners have easy access to a welcome refuge in political asylum. Regarding the complementary policies of maximizing the risks, Chapter VIII has mentioned the discussions held and the steps taken toward outlawing terrorism as such and thereby denying any political asylum to the diplonappers themselves, particularly as between the members of the O.A.S. Moreover, it has outlined some of the principal security measures which have been taken and which are being instituted in order both to deter any diplonapping attempts and to prevent their success if they occur. In all of these efforts it should be remembered that the ultimate success of these policies of prevention can best be assured if they are followed not only on a unilateral and national basis, but also bilaterally where most appropriate and through the multilateral agreements and institutions available. Diplonapping has become an international problem which deserves both international attention and international efforts for its control.

APPENDIX I

DIPLOMATIC KIDNAPPINGS (1968-1971) *

DATE	NAME	CITIZENSHIP	POSITION	HOST STATE	CATEGORY	RANSOM
8/28/68	John Gordan Mein	United States	Ambassador	Guatemala	I	None
9/4/69	Charles Burke Elbrick	United States	Ambassador	Brazil	II	15 Prisoners
10/5/69	Hermann Buff	Switzerland	First Secretary	Colombia	II	Money**
3/6/70	Sean M. Holly	United States	Political Secretary (Labor Attaché)	Guatemala	II	3 Prisoners
3/11/70	Nobuo Okuchi	Japan	Consul General	Brazil	II	5 Prisoners
3/24/70	Donald J. Crowley	United States	Air Attaché	Dominican Republic	II	20 Prisoners
3/24/70	Waldemar Sanchez	Paraguay	Consul	Argentina	III	None
3/29/70	Yuri Pivovarov	Soviet Union	Assistant Commercial Attaché	Argentina	I	None
3/31/70	Karl von Spreti	Germany	Ambassador	Guatemala	IV	None
4/5/70	Curtis C. Cutter	United States	Consul	Brazil	I	None
6/7/70	Morris Draper	United States	Political Secretary	Jordan	II or III	Uncertain
6/11/70	Ehrenfried von Holleben	Germany	Ambassador	Brazil	II	40 Prisoners
7/31/70	Dan A. Mitrione	United States	A.I.D. Advisor	Uruguay	IV	None
7/31/70	Aloysio Mares Diás Gomide	Brazil	Consul	Uruguay	II	Money**
8/7/70	Claude L. Fly	United States	Advisor	Uruguay	III	None (Heart Attack)
10/5/70	James R. Cross	United Kingdom	Consul	Canada	III	None
12/1/70	Eugen Beihl	Germany	Honorary Consul	Spain	II or III	Uncertain
12/7/70	Giovanni Enrico Bucher	Switzerland	Ambassador	Brazil	II	70 Prisoners
1/8/71	Geoffrey Jackson	United Kingdom	Ambassador	Uruguay	III	None***
5/17/71	Ephraim Elrom	Israel	Consul General	Turkey	IV	None
5/23/71	Stanley M. F. Sylvester	United Kingdom	Honorary Consul	Argentina	II	Food to Poor

Category I : Abortive Kidnapping Attempts.
Category II : Ransom Demands Met.
Category III: No Ransom, but Diplomat Released.
Category IV: No Ransom, and Diplomat Killed.

   * Exclusive of any kidnappings since 1/1/72.
  ** Amount not specified.
 *** 106 Tupamaro prisoners escaped.

CONVENTION TO PREVENT AND PUNISH THE ACTS OF TERRORISM TAKING THE FORM OF CRIMES AGAINST PERSONS AND RELATED EXTORTION THAT ARE OF INTERNATIONAL SIGNIFICANCE *

WHEREAS :

The defense of freedom and justice and respect for the fundamental rights of the individual that are recognized by the American Declaration of the Rights and Duties of Man and the Universal Declaration of Human Rights are primary duties of states;

The General Assembly of the Organization, in Resolution 4, of June 30, 1970, strongly condemned acts of terrorism, especially the kidnapping of persons and extortion in connection with that crime, which it declared to be serious common crimes;

Criminal acts against persons entitled to special protection under international law are occurring frequently, and those acts are of international significance because of the consquences that may flow from them for relations among states;

It is advisable to adopt general standards that will progressively develop international law as regards cooperation in the prevention and punishment of such acts; and

In the application of those standards the institution of asylum should be maintained and, likewise the principle of nonintervention should not be impaired,

THE MEMBER STATES OF THE ORGANIZATION OF AMERICAN STATES HAVE AGREED UPON THE FOLLOWING ARTICLES :

Article 1

The contracting states undertake to cooperate among themselves by taking all the measures that they may consider effective, under their own laws, and especially those established in this convention, to prevent and punish acts of terrorism, especially kidnapping, murder, and other assaults against the life or physical integrity of those persons to whom the state has the duty according to international law to give special protection, as well as extortion in connection with those crimes.

* OAS/OFFICIAL RECORDS/Ser. P/ENGLISH. Third Special Session, General Assembly, AG/doc. 88 rev. 1 corr. 1, 2 February 1971. Original: Spanish.

Article 2

For the purposes of this convention, kidnapping, murder, and other assaults against the life or personal integrity of those persons to whom the state has the duty to give special protection according to international law, as well as extortion in connection with those crimes, shall be considered common crimes of international significance, regardless of motive.

Article 3

Persons who have been charged or convicted for any of the crimes referred to in Article 2 of this convention shall be subject to extradition under the provisions of the extradition treaties in force between the parties or, in the case of states that do not make extradition dependent on the existence of a treaty, in accordance with their own laws.

In any case, it is the exclusive responsibility of the state under whose jurisdiction or protection such persons are located to determine the nature of the acts and decide whether the standards of this convention are applicable.

Article 4

Any person deprived of his freedom through the application of this convention shall enjoy the legal guarantees of due process.

Article 5

When extradition requested for one of the crimes specified in Article 2 is not in order because the person sought is a national of the requested state, or because of some other legal or constitutional impediment, that state is obliged to submit the case to its competent authorities for prosecution, as if the act had been committed in its terriory. The decision of these authorities shall be communicated to the state that requested extradition. In such proceedings, the obligation established in Article 4 shall be respected.

Article 6

None of the provisions of this convention shall be interpreted so as to impair the right of asylum.

Article 7

The contracting states undertake to include the crimes referred to in Article 2 of this convention among the punishable acts giving rise to extradition in any treaty on the subject to which they agree among themselves in the future. The contracting states that do not subject extradition to the existence of a treaty with the requesting state shall consider the crimes referred to in Article 2 of this convention as crimes giving rise to extradition, according to the conditions established by the laws of the requested state.

Article 8

To cooperate in preventing and punishing the crimes contemplated in Article 2 of this convention, the contracting states accept the following obligations:

a. To take all measures within their power, and in conformity with their own laws, to prevent and impede the preparation in their respective territories of the crimes mentioned in Article 2 that are to be carried out in the territory of another contracting state.
b. To exchange information and consider effective administrative measures for the purpose of protecting the persons to whom Article 2 of this convention refers.
c. To guarantee to every person deprived of his freedom through the application of this convention every right to defend himself.
d. To endeavor to have the criminal acts contemplated in this convention include in their penal laws, if not already so included.
e. To comply most expeditiously with the requests for extradition concerning the criminal acts contemplated in this convention.

Article 9

This convention shall remain open for signature by the member states of the Organization of American States, as well as by any other state that is member of the United Nations or any of its specialized agencies, or any state that is a party to the Statute of the International Court of Justice, or any other state that may be invited by the General Assembly of the Organization of American States to sign it.

Article 10

This convention shall be ratified by the signatory states in accordance with their respective constitutional procedures.

Article 11

The original instrument of this convention, the English, French, Portuguese, and Spanish texts of which are equally authentic, shall be deposited in the General Secretariat of the Organization of American States, which shall send certified copies to the signatory governments for purposes of ratification. The instruments of ratification shall be deposited in the General Secretariat of the Organization of American States, which shall notify the signatory governments of such deposit.

Article 12

This convention shall enter into force among the states that ratify it when they deposit their respective instruments of ratification.

Article 13

This convention shall remain in force indefinitely, but any of the contracting states may denounce it. The denunciation shall be transmitted to the General Secretariat of the Organization of American States, which shall notify the other contracting states thereof. One year following the denunciation, the convention shall cease to be in force for the denouncing state, but shall continue to be in force for the other contracting states.

STATEMENT OF PANAMA

The Delegation of Panama states for the record that nothing in this convention shall be interpreted to the effect that the right of asylum implies the right to request asylum from the United States authorities in the Panama Canal Zone, or that there is recognition of the right of the United States to grant asylum or political refuge in that part of the territory of the Republic of Panama that constitutes the Canal Zone.

IN WITNESS WHEREOF, the undersigned plenipotentiaries, having presented their full powers, which have been found to be in due and proper form, sign this convention on behalf of their respective governments, at the city of Washington this second day of Frebruary of the year one thousand nine hundred seventy-one.

THE CASE OF ISRAELI CONSUL GENERAL
EPHRAIM ELROM *

In addition to the kidnappings and murders of Ambassador Karl von Spreti in Guatemala and A.I.D. Advisor Dan A. Mitrione in Uruguay, the diplonapping of Israeli Consul General Ephraim Elrom provides a third example of cases in which no ransom was granted and the diplomat was consequently killed (Category IV). Four leftist terrorists kidnapped Consul General Elrom in Istanbul, Turkey, on May 17, 1971. The Turkish People's Liberation Army, also held accountable for the kidnapping of four U.S. servicemen in March, 1971 (see Chapter V), claimed responsibility for the abduction and demanded as ransom the release of all revolutionaries jailed in Turkey. They set a deadline of 5:00 P.M. on the 20th with the threat that if their demands were not met Mr. Elrom would "face a firing squad."

As in the case of the American airmen, the Turkish Government followed a hard-line policy toward the kidnappers and refused to accede to their ransom demands. The kidnapping took place in an atmosphere of extreme political tension and guerilla activity which had led the Government to the imposition of martial law in both Istanbul and Ankara in late April with charges of "a subversive conspiracy." Moreover, two trials of alleged members of the Liberation Army were currently being conducted and the Government indicated that some Turkish left-wing extremists were not only linked with the Popular Front for the Liberation of Palestine, but had actually received guerilla training with Palestinian guerilla organizations in Syria.

Following the Elrom kidnapping, the Turkish Government ordered the arrest of hundreds of leftists, including what the press referred to as 49 "of national prominence." The Deputy Premier for political affairs stated to the Senate that the Government had "no intention of bargaining with a handful of adventurers." The Turkish cabinet, meeting in extraordinary session, considered the adoption of a new law which would carry an automatic death penalty for kidnappers. Meanwhile, the Israeli

* Since the Elrom kidnapping occurred after the basic manuscript of this book had already been written, it was decided to include it here as Appendix III, rather than to attempt to incorporate it into the body of the text. The account is based largely on reports in the *New York Times,* May 18-31, 1971, and the *London Times,* June 1-4, 1971.

cabinet was also convened to discuss the kidnapping, and after a discussion of almost two hours, the Israeli Government expressed its confidence that the Turkish authorities would do all in their power to save Consul General Elrom. On May 18th a student member of the Turkish People's Liberation Army was arrested by Turkish security forces on suspicion of participation in the kidnapping.

Despite extensive security precautions, however, including the continuation of martial law in eleven provinces and the imposition of a 15-hour curfew and house to house search in Istanbul, Consul General Ephraim Elrom was shot to death on May 22nd, 1971. He was found in an apartment building in residential Istanbul, only some 500 yards from the Israeli Consulate General. The Turkish Premier, upon hearing of the news, stated that "The people who did this ... will be dealt with most severely. My Government is determined that Turkey will not become a country ruled by anarchists and terrorists." Within two days the Turkish Government asked the Parliament to approve a two-month extension of the April martial law; posters were put up throughout Istanbul with pictures of nine suspects wanted in connection with the kidnapping and murder of Consul General Elrom.

Meanwhile, by early June, it had become increasingly clear that through their terrorist excesses the urban guerillas were beginning to lose whatever public sympathy their proclaimed aims of a socialist revolution might otherwise have had. In addition to the murder of Mr. Elrom, two of the wanted men had kidnapped a 14-year-old girl as a new hostage;** moreover, some of the terrorists had been involved in such clearly nonpolitical crimes as robberies. Intellectuals who had supported the student Dev Geno (Revolutionary Youth) movement and its student demands for widespread national and academic reforms were soon revulsed by the terrorist tactics and not only publicly condemned these outright acts of violence, but did not protest against the security searches and arrests subsequently conducted by the Turkish Army. In contrast to the police forces which did not enjoy much popular support in Turkey, the Turkish Army and its leaders have generally commanded greater respect.

Non-selective and wanton terrorism, as pointed out in Chapter I, may thus come to alienate the very populace which it aims to convert and

---

** The youths were reported to have offered to free the girl in exchange for passports and safe conduct out of the country; she was ultimately rescued on June 1st after a gunfight in which one of the guerillas was killed and the other wounded.

build upon. If the government responds by excessively repressive measures of its own, the guerillas may retain and indeed even increase the popular support they may have nurtured. But if their grievances are not deeply felt or equally shared by significantly large and influential segments of the population, or if the government reacts firmly, but in moderate proportion to counter the threat posed to a modicum of national order and public security, then the guerillas may soon find themselves isolated from their own compatriots. Just as the kidnappings and murders of diplomats have struck at the foundations of international diplomatic intercourse and have thus provoked international outcry and combined action against them, so also the philosophy of terrorism which espouses such acts and contributes to the political milieu within which they can occur has itself become the object of both international and national concern and counter-action.

DRAFT ARTICLES ON THE PREVENTION AND PUNISHMENT OF CRIMES AGAINST DIPLOMATIC AGENTS AND OTHER INTERNATIONALLY PROTECTED PERSONS *

Article 1

For the purposes of the present articles:

1. "Internationally protected person" means:

(a) a Head of State or a Head of Government, whenever he is in a foreign State, as well as members of his family who accompany him;

(b) any official of either a State or an international organization who is entitled, pursuant to general international law or an international agreement, to special protection for or because of the performance of functions on behalf of his State or international organization, as well as members of his family who are likewise entitled to special protection.

2. "Alleged offender" means a person as to whom there are grounds to believe that he has committed one or more of the crimes set forth in article 2.

3. "International organization" means an intergovernmental organization.

Article 2

1. The intentional commission, regardless of motive, of:

(a) a violent attack upon the person or liberty of an internationally protected person;

(b) a violent attack upon the official premises or the private accommodation of an internationally protected person likely to endanger his person or liberty;

(c) a threat to commit any such attack;

(d) an attempt to commit any such attack; and

(e) participation as an accomplice in any such attack,

* International Law Commission: Draft Articles on the Prevention and Punishment of Crimes against Diplomats. Reproduced from the *Report of the International Law Commission on the Work of Its Twenty-fourth Session* (May 2 - July 7, 1972), U.N. Document A/8710 of July 22, 1972. In *International Legal Materials: Current Documents,* Vol. XI, No. 5 (September, 1972), pp. 977-999.

shall be made by each State Party a crime under its internal law, whether the commission of the crime occurs within or outside of its territory.

2. Each State Party shall make these crimes punishable by severe penalties which take into account the aggravated nature of the offence.

3. Each State Party shall take such measures as may be necessary to establish its jurisdiction over these crimes.

Article 3

States Party shall co-operate in the prevention of the crimes set forth in article 2 by:

(a) taking measures to prevent the preparation in their respective territories for the commission of those crimes either in their own or in other territories;

(b) exchanging information and co-ordinating the taking of administrative measures to prevent the commission of those crimes.

Article 4

The State Party in which one or more of the crimes set forth in article 2 have been committed shall, if it has reason to believe an alleged offender has fled from its territory, communicate to all other States Party all the pertinent facts regarding the crime committed and all available information regarding the identity of the alleged offender.

Article 5

1. The State Party in whose territory the alleged offender is present shall take the appropriate measures under its internal law so as to ensure his presence for prosecution or extradition. Such measures shall be immediately notified to the State where the crime was committed, the State or States of which the alleged offender is a national, the State or States of which the internationally protected person concerned is a national and all interested States.

2. Any person regarding whom the measures referred to in paragraph 1 of this article are being taken shall be entitled to communicate immediately with the nearest appropriate representative of the State of which he is a national and to be visited by a representative of that State.

Article 6

The State Party in whose territory the alleged offender is present shall, if it does not extradite him, submit, without exception whatsoever and without undue delay, the case to its competent authorities for the purpose of prosecution, through proceedings in accordance with the laws of that State.

Article 7

1. To the extent that the crimes set forth in article 2 are not listed as extraditable offences in any extradition treaty existing between States Party they shall be deemed to have been included as such therein. States Party undertake to include those crimes as extraditable offences in every future extradition treaty to be concluded between them.

2. If a State Party which makes extradition conditional on the existence of a treaty receives a request for extradition from another State Party with which it has no extradition treaty, it may, if it decides to extradite, consider the present articles as the legal basis for extradition in respect of the crimes. Extradition shall be subject to the procedural provisions of the law of the requested State.

3. States Party which do not make extradition conditional on the existence of a treaty shall recognize the crimes as extraditable offences between themselves subject to the procedural provisions of the law of the requested State.

4. An extradition request from the State in which the crimes were committed shall have priority over other such requests if received by the State Party in whose territory the alleged offender has been found within six months after the communication required under paragraph 1 of article 5 has been made.

Article 8

Any person regarding whom proceedings are being carried out in connexion with any of the crimes set forth in article 2 shall be guaranteed fair treatment at all stages of the proceedings.

Article 9

The statutory limitation as to the time within which prosecution may be instituted for the crimes set forth in article 2 shall be, in each State Party, that fixed for the most serious crimes under its internal law.

Article 10

1. States Party shall afford one another the greatest measure of assistance in connexion with criminal proceedings brought in respect of the crimes set forth in article 2, including the supply of all evidence at their disposal necessary for the proceedings.

2. The provisions of paragraph 1 of this article shall not affect obligations concerning mutual judicial assistance embodied in any other treaty.

Article 11

The final outcome of the legal proceedings regarding the alleged offender shall be communicated by the State Party where the proceedings are conducted to the Secretary-General of the United Nations, who shall transmit the information to the other States Party.

Article 12

Alternative A

1. Any dispute between the Parties arising out of the application or interpretation of the present articles that is not settled through negotiation may be brought by any State party to the dispute before a conciliation Commission to be constituted in accordance with the provisions of this article by the giving of written notice to the other State or States party to the dispute and to the Secretary-General of the United Nations.

2. A conciliation commission will be composed of three members. One member shall be appointed by each party to the dispute. If there is more than one party on either side of the dispute they shall jointly appoint a member of the conciliation Commission. These two appointments shall be made within two months of the written notice referred to in paragraph 1. The third member, the Chairman, shall be chosen by the other two members.

3. If either side has failed to appoint its member within the time-limit referred to in paragraph 2, the Secretary-General shall appoint such member within a further period of two months. If no agreement is reached on the choice of the Chairman within five months of the written notice referred to in paragraph 1, the Secretary-General shall within the further period of one month appoint as the Chairman a qualified jurist who is not a national of any State party to the dispute.

4.   Any vacancy shall be filled in the same manner as the original appointment was made.

5.   The commission shall establish its own rules of procedure and shall reach its decisions and recommendations by a majority vote. It shall be competent to ask any organ that is authorized by or in accordance with the Charter of the United Nations to request an advisory opinion from the International Court of Justice to make such a request regarding the interpretation or application of the present articles.

6.   If the commission is unable to obtain an agreement among the parties on a settlement of the dispute within six months of its initial meeting, it shall prepare as soon as possible a report of its proceedings and transmit it to the parties and to the depositary. The report shall include the commission's conclusions upon the facts and questions of law and the recommendations it has submitted to the parties in order to facilitate a settlement of the dispute. The six months time-limit may be extended by decision of the commission.

7.   This article is without prejudice to provisions concerning the settlement of disputes contained in international agreements in force between States.

Alternative B

1.   Any dispute between two or more Parties concerning the interpretation or application of the present articles which cannot be settled through negotiation, shall, at the request of one of them, be submitted to arbitration. If within six months from the date of the request for arbitration the Parties are unable to agree on the organization of the arbitration, any one of those Parties may refer the dispute to the International Court of Justice by request in conformity with the Statute of the Court.

2.   Each Party may at the time of signature or ratification of these articles or accession thereto, declare that it does not consider itself bound by the preceding paragraph. The other Parties shall not be bound by the preceding paragraph with respect to any Parties having made such a reservation.

3.   Any Party having made a reservation in accordance with the preceding paragraph may at any time withdraw this reservation by notification to the Depositary Governments.

INDEX